Unity 5 From Zero to Proficiency (Foundations)

A step-by-step guide to creating your first game.

Patrick Felicia

UNITY 5 FROM ZERO TO PROFICIENCY

(FOUNDATIONS)

First published: October 2015

Published by Patrick Felicia

CREDITS

Author: Patrick Felicia

ABOUT THE AUTHOR

Patrick Felicia is a lecturer and researcher at Waterford Institute of Technology, where he teaches and supervises undergraduate and postgraduate students. He obtained his MSc in Multimedia Technology in 2003 and PhD in Computer Science in 2009 from University College Cork, Ireland. He has published several books and articles on the use of video games for educational purposes, including the Handbook of Research on Improving Learning and Motivation through Educational Games: Multidisciplinary Approaches (published by IGI), and Digital Games in Schools: a Handbook for Teachers, published by European Schoolnet. Patrick is also the Editor-in-chief of the International Journal of Game-Based Learning (IJGBL), and the Conference Director of the Irish Symposium on Game-Based Learning, a popular conference on games and learning organized throughout Ireland.

SUPPORT AND RESOURCES FOR THIS BOOK

So that you can complete the project presented in this book seamlessly, a website has been setup, and it includes all the material you need to complete the project presented in the next chapters (e.g., textures or solutions for each chapter), as well as bonus material.

To avail of this content, you can open the link:

`http://www.learntocreategames.com/learn-unity-ebook/`.

`http://www.learntocreategames.com` also provides you with the opportunity to subscribe to a newsletter, obtain exclusive discounts and offers on new books, and gain access to video tutorials on creating games.

Why should you subscribe?

- Be the first to be notified of new resources available.

- Receive regular updates and tutorials on creating games.

- Receive a newsletter with tips and hints on game development.

This book is dedicated to Helena

TABLE OF CONTENTS

PREFACE

After teaching Unity for over 4 years, I always thought it could be great to find a book that could get my students started on Unity in a few hours and that showed them how to master the core functionalities offered by this fantastic software.

Many of the books that I found were too short and did not provide enough details on the why behind the actions recommended and taken; other books were highly theoretical, and I found they lacked practicality and would not get my students' full attention. In addition, I often found that game development may be preferred by those with a programming background but that those with an Arts background, even if they wanted to get to know how to create games, often had to face the issue of learning to code for the first time.

As a result, I started to consider a format that would cover both: be approachable (even to the students with no programming background), keep students highly motivated and involved using an interesting project, cover the core functionalities available in Unity to get started on game programming, provide answers to common questions, and also provide, if need be, a considerable amount of details for some topics.

This book series entitled **From Zero to Proficiency** does just this. In this book series, you have the opportunity to play around with Unity's core features, and essentially those that will make it possible to create an interesting 3D game rapidly. After reading this book series, you should find it easier to use Unity and its core functionalities.

This book series assumes no prior knowledge on the part of the reader, and it will get you started on Unity so that you quickly master all the wonderful features that this software provides by going through an easy learning curve. By completing each chapter, and following step-by-step instructions, you will progressively improve your skills, become more proficient in Unity, and create a survival game using Unity's core features in terms of programming (C# and JavaScript), game design, and drag and drop features.

In addition to understanding and being able to master Unity's core features, you will also create a game that includes many of the common techniques found in video games, including: level design, object creation, textures, collection detection, lights, weapon creation, character animations, particles, artificial intelligence, and menus.

Throughout this book series, you will create a game that includes both indoor and outdoor environments where the player needs to finds its way out of the former through tunnels, escalators, traps, and other challenges, avoid or eliminate enemies using weapons (i.e., gun or grenades), drive a car or pilot an aircraft.

You will learn how to create customized menus and simple user interfaces using Unity's new UI system, and animate and give (artificial) intelligence to Non-Player Characters (NPCs) who will be able to follow your character using Mecanim and Navmesh navigation.

Finally you will also get to export your game for the web at the different stages of the books, so that you can share it with friends and get some feedback.

CONTENT COVERED BY THIS BOOK

Chapter 1, The Benefits of Using Unity, provides general information on game engines and explains why you should use such software, and how, by using Unity more specifically, you can create games seamlessly.

Chapter 2, Installing Unity and Becoming Familiar with the Interface, takes you through the very first steps of installing Unity and becoming familiar with the interface. It will also show you the different shortcuts necessary to navigate through scenes and projects in Unity.

Chapter 3, Creating and Exporting your First Scene, gets you to create and export your first scene by combining built-in objects. You will learn how to manage objects, apply textures and colors, and transform objects to create a simple scene.

Chapter 4, Transforming Built-in Objects to Create an Indoor Scene, explains how you can create an indoor scene (i.e., a maze) with built-in shapes. You will also work with and manage lights in your scene to set the atmosphere and navigate through the scene with a First-Person Controller.

Chapter 5, Creating an outdoor Scene with Unity's Built-in Terrain Generator, explains how you can create an outdoor scene with water, hills, sandy beaches and palm trees using Unity's built-in assets. You will also be able to add and control a car and a plane.

Chapter 6 provides answers to frequently asked questions based on specific themes and topics (e.g., assets creation or transformations).

Chapter 7 summarizes the topics covered in this book and also provides useful information if you would like to progress further with this book series.

WHAT YOU NEED TO USE THIS BOOK

To complete the project presented in this book, you only need Unity 5.0 (or a more recent version) and to also ensure that your computer and its operating system comply with Unity's requirements. Unity can be downloaded from the official website (http://www.unity3d.com/download), and before downloading, you can check that your computer is up to scratch on the following page: http://www.unity3d.com/unity/system-requirements. At the time of writing this book, the following operating systems are supported by Unity for development: Windows XP (i.e., SP2+, 7 SP1+), Windows 8, and Mac OS X 10.6+. In terms of graphics card, most cards produced after 2004 should be suitable.

In terms of computer skills, all knowledge introduced in this book will assume no prior programming experience from the reader. This book does not include any scripting (this will be introduced in the second book in the series). So for now, you only need to be able to perform common computer tasks such as downloading items, opening and saving files, and be comfortable with dragging and dropping items and typing.

WHO THIS BOOK IS FOR

If you can answer **yes** to all these questions, then this book is for you:

1. Are you a total beginner in Unity or programming?

2. Would you like to become proficient in the core functionalities offered by Unity?

3. Would you like to teach students or help your child to understand how to create games?

4. Would you like to start creating great games?

5. Although you may have had some prior exposure to Unity, would you like to delve more into Unity and understand its core functionalities in more detail?

WHO THIS BOOK IS NOT FOR

If you can answer yes to all these questions, then this book is **not** for you:

1. Can you already easily create a 3D game with Unity with built-in objects, controllers, cameras, lights, and terrains?

2. Are you looking for a reference book on Unity programming?

3. Are you an experienced (or at least advanced) Unity user?

If you can answer yes to all three questions, you may instead look for the next books in the series. To see the content and topics covered by these books, you can check the official website (www.learntocreategames.com/learn-unity-ebook).

HOW YOU WILL LEARN FROM THIS BOOK

Because all students learn differently and have different expectations of a course, this book is designed to ensure that all readers find a learning mode that suits them. Therefore, it includes the following:

- A list of the learning objectives at the start of each chapter so that readers have a snapshot of the skills that will be covered.

- Each section includes an overview of the activities covered.

- Many of the activities are step-by-step, and learners are also given the opportunity to engage in deeper learning and problem-solving skills through the challenges offered at the end of each chapter.

- Each chapter ends-up with a quiz and challenges through which you can put your skills (and knowledge acquired) into practice, and see how much you know.

- The book focuses on the core skills that you need; some sections also go into more detail; however, once concepts have been explained, links are provided to additional resources, where necessary.

FORMAT OF EACH CHAPTER AND WRITING CONVENTIONS

Throughout this book, and to make reading and learning easier, text formatting and icons will be used to highlight parts of the information provided and make it more readable.

The full solution for the project presented in this book is available for download on the official website (http://www.learntocreategames.com/learn-unity-ebook). So if you need to skip a section, you can do so; you can also download the solution for the previous chapter that you have skipped.

SPECIAL NOTES

Each chapter includes resource sections so that you can further your understanding and mastery of Unity; these include:

- A quiz for each chapter: these quizzes usually include 10 questions that test your knowledge of the topics covered throughout the chapter. The solutions are provided on the companion website.

- A checklist: it consists of between 5 and 10 key concepts and skills that you need to be comfortable with before progressing to the next chapter.

- Challenges: each chapter includes a challenge section where you are asked to combine your skills to solve a particular problem.

Author's notes appear as described below:

Author's suggestions appear in this box.

Checklists that include the important points covered in the chapter appear as described below:

- Item1 for check list

- Item2 for check list

- Item3 for check list

HOW CAN YOU LEARN BEST FROM THIS BOOK

- **Talk to your friends about what you are doing.**

  We often think that we understand a topic until we have to explain it to friends and answer their questions. By explaining your different projects, what you just learned will become clearer to you.

- **Do the exercises.**

  All chapters include exercises that will help you to learn by doing. In other words, by completing these exercises, you will be able to better understand the topic and gain practical skills (i.e., rather than just reading).

- **Don't be afraid of making mistakes.**

  I usually tell my students that making mistakes is part of the learning process; the more mistakes you make and the more opportunities you have for learning. At the start, you may find the errors disconcerting, or that the engine does not work as expected until you understand what went wrong.

- **Export your games early.**

  It is always great to build and export your first game. Even if it is rather simple, it is always good to see it in a browser and to be able to share it with you friends.

- **Learn in chunks.**

  It may be disconcerting to go through five or six chapters straight, as it may lower your motivation. Instead, give yourself enough time to learn, go at your own pace, and learn in small units (e.g., between 15 and 20 minutes per day). This will do at least two things for you: it will give your brain the time to "digest" the information that you have just learned, so that you can start fresh the following day. It will also make sure that you don't "burn-out" and that you keep your motivation levels high.

FEEDBACK

While I have done everything possible to produce a book of high quality and value, I always appreciate feedback from readers so that the book can be improved accordingly. If you would like to give feedback, you can email me at `learntocreategames@gmail.com`.

DOWNLOADING THE SOLUTIONS FOR THE BOOK

You can download the solutions for this book after creating a free online account at www.learntocreategames.com/learn-unity-ebook. Once you have registered, a link to the files will be sent to you automatically.

IMPROVING THE BOOK

Although great care was taken in checking the content of this book, I am human, and some errors could remain in the book. As a result, it would be great if you could let me know of any issue or error you may have come across in this book, so that it can be solved and the book updated accordingly. To report an error, you can email me (learntocreategames@gmail.com) with the following information:

- Name of the book.

- The page where the error was detected.

- Describe the error and also what you think the correction should be.

Once your email is received, the error will be checked, and, in the case of a valid error, it will be corrected and the book page will be updated to reflect the changes accordingly.

SUPPORTING THE AUTHOR

A lot of work has gone into this book and it is the fruit of long hours of preparation, brainstorming, and finally writing. As a result, I would ask that you do not distribute any illegal copies of this book.

This means that if a friend wants a copy of this book, s/he will have to buy it through the official channels (i.e., through Amazon, lulu.com, or the book's official website: `www.learntocreategames.com/learn-unity-ebook`).

If some of your friends are interested in the book, you can refer them to the book's official website (`http://www.learntocreategames.com/learn-unity-ebook`) where they can either buy the book, enter a monthly draw to be in for a chance of receiving a free copy of the book, or to be notified of future promotional offers.

1

THE BENEFITS OF USING UNITY

This chapter is an introduction to game engines and Unity, and it explains the benefits brought by game engines, and more specifically how Unity can help you to create games seamlessly. The most recent features are explained, and examples of games created in Unity are also given so that you can evaluate the potential of this game engine.

If you already know of the benefits of Unity and game engines in general, you can skip to the next chapter.

After completing this section, you should be able to:

- Understand the concept of game engines.

- Know the features introduced by Unity 5.

- Understand the benefits of using Unity.

WHAT IS A GAME ENGINE AND SHOULD YOU USE ONE?

Unity is a software that makes it possible to create video games without knowing some of the underlying technologies of game development, so that potential game developers only need to focus on the game mechanics and employ a high-level approach to creating games using programming and scripting languages such as C# or JavaScript. The term high-level here refers to the fact that, when you create a game with a game engine, you don't need to worry about how the software will render the game or how it will communicate with the graphics card to optimize the speed of your game. So using a game engine would generally offer the following features and benefits:

- Accelerated development: game engines make it possible to focus on the game mechanics. Because built-in libraries are available for common mechanics and features, these do not need to be rebuilt from scratch, and programmers can use them straightaway and save time (e.g., for the user interface or the artificial intelligence).

- Integrated Development Environment (IDE): an IDE helps to create, compile, and manage your code, and includes some useful tools that make development and debugging more efficient.

- Graphical User Interface (GUI): while some game engines are based on libraries, most common game engines make it possible for users to create objects seamlessly and to perform common tasks such as transforming, texturing, and animating, through drag and drop features. Another advantage of such software is that you can understand and preview how the game will look without having to compile the code (e.g., through scenes).

- Multi-platform deployment: with common game engines, it is possible to export the game you have created to several platforms with the click of a button (e.g., for the web, iOS, or Android) without having to recode the entire game.

ADVANTAGES OF USING UNITY

There are several game engines available out there; however, Unity has proven to be one of the best engines. It has been used by game developers for several years and has been employed to produce successful 3D and 2D games. Several of these title can be seen on Unity's website (`http://unity3d.com/gallery/made-with-unity/game-list`).

With Unity, you can create 2D or 3D games and produce several types of game genres including First-Person Shooters (FPS), Massive Multiplayer Online Role Playing Games (MMORPG), casual games, adventure games, and much more.

In addition to being able to create high-quality games with an easy-to-use interface, Unity makes it possible to export games to a wide range of platforms, including Android, iOS, Windows Phone 8, Mac, Linux, PS3, or XBOX360.

Unity includes all the necessary tools that you need to create great games and it also simplifies the application of useful techniques to improve the quality of your game. For example, it includes Mono Develop, an IDE that will help you to code faster, built-in Artificial Intelligence (AI) modules (e.g., navmesh navigation) that you can use with no prior knowledge of AI, lights, built-in objects, or a finite state machine that you can apply to your characters for customized behaviors.

Finally, in order to control the game, you can use high-level programming and scripting languages such as Boo, C# or JavaScript. This is useful for those who have already been exposed to one of these languages to transfer their skills to game programming in Unity. It also provides programmers with a choice depending on their level of proficiency. For example, beginners may prefer JavaScript, while more advanced coders may prefer to use C# (i.e., for those with prior experience of Object Oriented Programming).

NOVELTIES INTRODUCED IN UNITY 4.6 AND 5.0

Currently, Unity is in version 5. While the Unity team is consistently working hard to improve the features and functionalities included within, the software has been through a steady pace of changes and improvements since its first launch. Bugs are being fixed quickly and the Unity team is always looking into making this software easier to use and more efficient.

While subsequent versions will, without a doubt, introduce interesting new features, most of the skills and knowledge that you will acquire in this book should still be relevant.

Unity 4 introduced much-awaited exciting features such as Mecanim (i.e., for character animations). Unity 4.6 also marked an important step for users as it included Unity UI, a feature that makes it possible to create smoother, dynamic and more intuitive Graphical User Interfaces (GUI) for your game. Meanwhile, amongst other things, previously premium features found in version 4.x (e.g., navmesh and iOS or Android export) are now available for free in Unity 5 personal edition.

Unity 5.0 was released in 2015 and has brought significant changes in both the way the software is licensed and its features. From Unity 5.0 onwards, the software comes into two main versions: the personal edition and the professional edition. For the former, all the features of the engine are available. In the latter, you gain access to additional features such as customizable splash screen, team licenses, or game performance reporting. In terms of features, Unity 5.0 introduces a wide range of features that will make your game look more realistic and polished, including global illumination (for improved illumination when using both static and dynamic objects), the Audio Mixer or export to WebGL.

As you can see, there is much to learn in Unity and we will focus on Unity's core technologies in this book series.

- 5 -

LEVEL ROUNDUP

Summary

This chapter has described some of the reasons why you should use Unity and some of its core functionalities. You have also discovered the concept of game engine, the benefits brought by game engines, and how Unity can specifically make it easier for you to get started with game development.

2

INSTALLING UNITY AND BECOMING FAMILIAR WITH THE INTERFACE

This chapter helps you to progressively become familiar with Unity by explaining and illustrating how to install this software, and how the different views and core features can be employed. You will also learn to create your first project and scene, using predefined objects such as boxes. After learning the features of the different views available in Unity, you will learn how to navigate through a scene (to look at objects), before creating you very first game with built-in objects and applying colors and textures.

After completing this section, you should be able to:

- Be more confortable with Unity's interface.

- Understand the role and location of the different views in Unity.

- Understand the role of colliders.

- Add and configure cameras and lights.

- Know and use shortcuts to manipulate objects (e.g., move, scale, resize, duplicate, or delete) and move the view accordingly (e.g., pan or rotate).

- Use the **Inspector** view.

- Create and apply colors and textures to objects.

- Create and combine simple built-in shapes.

- Know how to search for and organize assets in your game efficiently.

- Navigate through your scene and see it from both first- and third-person views.

DOWNLOADING UNITY

Now that you have had an overview of Unity and game engines, it is time for us to start using Unity. Unity is available for download, for free, from the Unity website and the next steps will show you how to download it:

1. Open the following link: `http://unity3d.com/unity/system-requirements`. This will help you to check that your computer complies with Unity's requirements.

2. Once you have checked the requirements, we can download Unity by opening the following page: `http://unity3d.com/get-unity/download?ref=personal`

3. Once the page is opened, a link to the current version of Unity is provided (i.e., the installer). This page will automatically detect whether you computer is running Mac OS X or Windows, and by clicking on the link, the corresponding installer will be downloaded to your computer (i.e., *.dmg* for MacOSX or *.exe* for Windows), as described on the next figure. Note that direct links to either version are available in Unity's archive (`http://unity3d.com/get-unity/download/archive`).

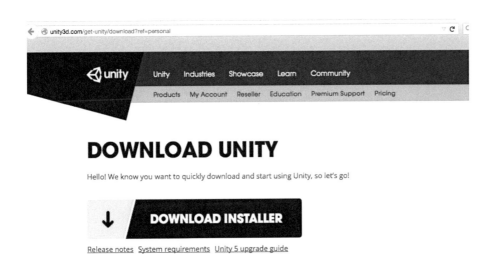

Figure 2-1: Downloading Unity from the official website

It is possible to download previous versions of Unity from Unity's archive (`http://unity3d.com/get-unity/download/archive`). This may be useful if you work from two different locations for your Unity project and if each computer has a different version of Unity installed. If this is the case, you will be able to open projects built with an older version of Unity with a new version of Unity (e.g., a project initially created with Unity 4.x can be opened with Unity 5.x); however, after opening a project that was created with an older version of Unity, this project is converted to the new version of Unity and can no more be opened with the previous version (i.e., a project initially created with Unity 4.x, and then opened with Unity 5.x can't be opened anymore with Unity 4.x). You may also backup you project before any file conversion, for safety.

Once we have downloaded Unity, we can launch the installer and follow the onscreen instructions. Once the software is installed, you can progress to the next section.

LAUNCHING UNITY

Once you have successfully installed Unity, we can now launch it. Upon the first time you open Unity, you may need to provide your email address, so that you can receive regular updates from the Unity team. This should be really useful to keep up-to-date with major announcements for this software. You may also be asked whether you would like to activate the Pro version; however, for the purpose of this tutorial, you only need to use the free version (i.e., personal edition).

After having provided your email details as well as choosing the free version of the software, we can start to enjoy Unity.

After launching Unity, the following window appears:

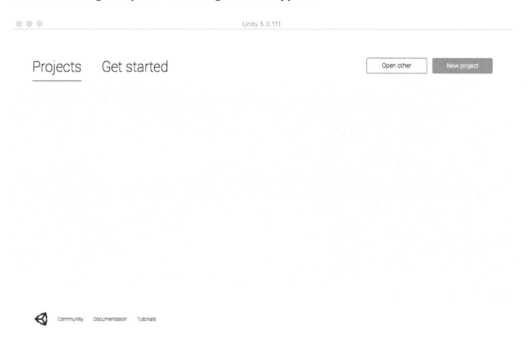

Figure 2-2: Launching Unity for the first time

The previous figure shows a window labeled **Projects** that lists all projects that you have been working on previously (i.e., empty for now). If you click on the label **Get Started**, you can access a welcome video from the Unity Team that briefly describes the new features introduced by this version. You may also notice three buttons at the bottom of the window, labeled **Community**, **Documentation**, and **Tutorials**, which will take you to the relevant resources on the Unity website also. (i.e., Unity forums, the official documentation for Unity, or official Unity tutorials).

Let's press the button labeled **New Project** to create a new project. The following window should appear:

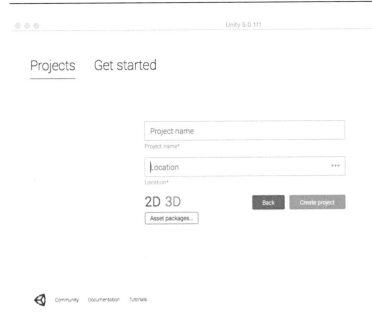

Figure 2-3: Creating a new project

In this window, we will specify a name for our project, as well as a location.

- In the section **Project Name**: type a name of your choice, for example **myFirstProject**.

- In the **Location** section: click on the three dots located to the right of the label **Location** and select where on your hard drive you would like to save the project.

- **2D/3D**: for this project, we will be using a three-dimensional environment; therefore, we will click on the **3D** icon. As we will see later, you can create both 2D and 3D games with Unity, and projects are setup accordingly.

- **Assets/Packages**: we will leave this option as default, as we will identify later the assets that will be necessary for our first project.

- Once you have entered this information, you can now click on the button labeled **Create Project**.

When Unity starts-up, a window labeled **Unity Editor Update Check** appears. This window, illustrated below, is there to check whether you have the latest version of Unity and to let you know of any recent updates available. If an update is necessary, you can install it; if you would prefer not to see this message displayed every time you start Unity, you can uncheck the corresponding box labeled **Check for Updates** accordingly.

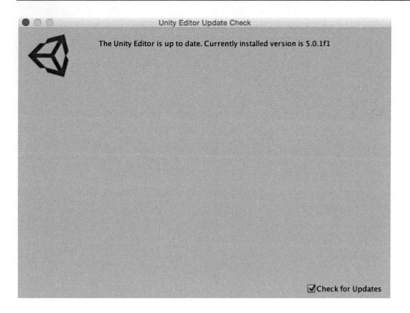

Figure 2-4: Automatically checking for Unity updates

Unity provides links to official forums and documentation from the main (i.e., top) menu: **Help | Unity Forums** or **Help | Unity Manual.**

UNDERSTANDING AND BECOMING FAMILIAR WITH THE INTERFACE

As for any major version of Unity, once you open this software for the first time, a project is already loaded and ready to play. This project usually illustrates and brings forward the most interesting features available in the latest version. In Unity 5.x, this project is called *Viking Village* and includes a very interesting and fun level to play and to discover. All projects delivered in versions 1, 2, 3 and 4 of Unity are also available through the **Assets Store**, which is available from Unity by selecting **Window | Assets Store** from the main menu. At this point in time, although some demo levels have been released for Unity 5.0, an official playable level has not been released yet. This is the reason why we will be using the demo project called *Viking Village* in the next sections.

After launching Unity, we can notice that it includes several windows organized in a (default) layout. Each of these windows includes a label (usually in the top-left corner) of the window, and all can be moved around, if necessary, by either changing the layout (**Window | Layouts | ...**) or by dragging and dropping the corresponding tab for a window (this will move the view to where you would like it to appear within the window). In the default layout, the following views appear onscreen (as described in the next screenshot, clockwise from the top left corner):

1. The **Hierarchy** window (the corresponding shortcut is *CTRL+4*): this window or view lists all the objects currently present in your scene; these could include, for example, basic shapes, 3D characters, or terrains. This view also makes it possible to identify a hierarchy between objects; for example, we can see in this view if some objects have children or parents (we will explore this concept later).

2. The **Scene** view (*CTRL+1*): this window displays the content of a scene (or the item listed in the **Hierarchy** view) so that you can visualize them and modify them accordingly using the mouse (e.g., move, scale, etc.).

3. The **Game** view (*CTRL+2*): this window makes it possible to visualize the scene as it will appear in the game (i.e., through the lenses of the active camera).

4. The **Inspector** view (*CTRL+3*): this window displays information (i.e., properties) on the object currently selected.

5. The **Console** window (*SHIFT+CTRL+C*): this window displays messages either printed from the code by the user (using keywords) or by Unity. These include warnings or error messages related to your project or code.

6. The **Project** window (*CTRL+5*): this window includes all the assets available and used for your project. These include 3D models, sounds, or textures.

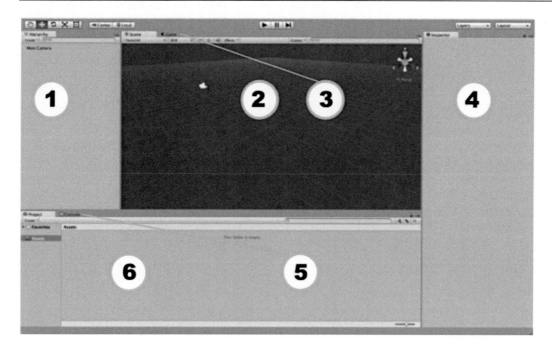

Figure 2-5: Main windows and views in Unity

THE SCENE VIEW

We will use this view to create and visualize the scene for our game. When you create a project, you can include several scenes within. A scene is comparable to a level, and scenes that are included in the same project can share similar resources, so that assets are imported once and shared across (or used in) all scenes. The **Scene** and **Game** views are displayed in the same window, and both are represented by a corresponding tab. By default, the **Scene** view is active; however, it is possible to switch to the **Game** view by clicking on the tab labeled **Game**. For example, if we click successively on the **Game** and **Scene** tabs, we can see the view from both the perspectives of your eyes (i.e., scene view) and the active camera present in the scene (**Game** view) as illustrated in the next figures.

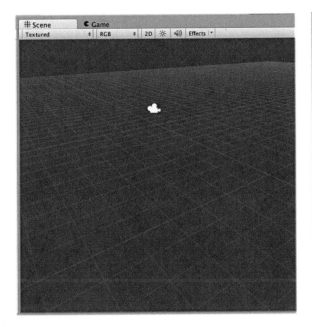

Figure 2-6: The Scene view

Figure 2-7: The Game view

Note that you can also rearrange the layout to be able to, for example, see both the **Scene** and **Game** views simultaneously. We could drag and drop the **Game** tab beside the **Console** tab to obtain the layout described on the next figure.

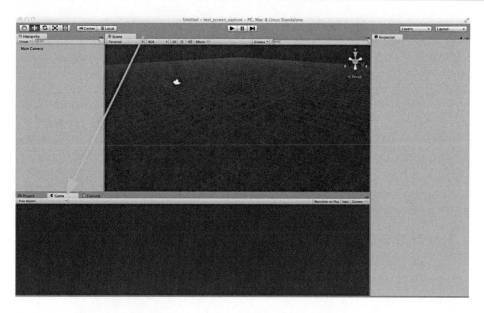

Figure 2-8: Changing the layout to display both Game and Scene views

DISCOVERING AND NAVIGATING THROUGH THE SCENE

So that you can navigate easily in the current scene, several shortcuts and navigation modes are available. These make it possible to navigate through your scene just as you would in a First-Person Shooter or to literally "Fly" through your scene. You can also zoom-in and zoom-out to focus on particular areas or objects, look around (i.e., using mouse look) or pan the view to focus on a specific part of the scene. The main modes of navigation are provided in the next table; however, we will look into these in more detail in the next section as we will be experimenting with them to explore (and modify) an existing scene.

Table 1: Navigation shortcuts

Navigation	Key or Mouse Combination
Activate Fly Mode	Keep MRB (Mouse Right Button) pressed.
Accelerate	Press Shift (in walk mode).
Move in four directions (left, right, forward and back)	Press W, A, S, or D.
Float Up and Down	Press Q or E (in fly mode).
Look around	Press *ALT* and drag the mouse left, right, forward or back.
Zoom in/out	Move the mouse wheel.
Pan the view	Press Q (to activate the hand tool) then drag and drop the mouse.

For example, in the default navigation mode, you can "walk" through the scene using the arrow keys (up, down, left and right). In the "flight" mode, which can be activated by pressing and holding the Mouse Right Button (MRB), we can navigate using the *W, A, S* and *D* keys and also look around us by dragging the mouse in the direction we would like to look (i.e., left, right, up and down) and also float up and down using the keys *Q* and *E*. As you can see, both modes are very useful to navigate through your scene and to visualize all its elements. In addition, you can also choose to display the scene along a particular axis (x, y, or z) using the **gizmo** that is displayed in the top-right corner of the **Scene** view as described on the next figure.

Figure 2-9: Gizmo

The gizmo available in the **Scene** view includes three axes that are color-coded: x (in red), y (in green) and z (in blue). By clicking on any of these axes (or corresponding letters), the scene will be seen accordingly (i.e., through the x-, y-, or z-axis).

If you are not familiar with 3D axes: **x**, and **z** usually refer to the width and depth, while **y** refers to the height. By default, in Unity, the z-axis is pointing towards the screen if the x-axis is pointing to the right and the y-axis is pointing upwards. This is often referred as a left-handed coordinate system.

Also note that by clicking on the middle of the gizmo (white box), we can switch between isometric and perspective views.

In addition to the navigation tools, Unity also offers ways to focus on a particular object by rotating around a specific point (i.e., by pressing the *ALT* key and dragging the mouse to the left, right, up or down), or double-clicking on an object (i.e., in the **Scene** or **Hierarchy** view), so that the camera in the **Scene** view is focused on this object (this can also be achieved by selecting the object in either the **Scene** or **Hierarchy** view and pressing *SHIFT+ F*), or by zooming-in and out (i.e., scrolling the mouse wheel forward or back).

While the shortcuts and keys described in this section should get you started with Unity and make it possible for you to navigate through your scene easily, there are, obviously, many more shortcuts that you could use, but that will not be presented in this book. Instead, you may look for and find these in the official documentation that is available both offline (using the top menu: **Help | Unity Manual** then select the sections **Unity Overview | Unity Basics | Learning the Interface | Scene View**) and online (http://docs.unity3d.com/Documentation/Manual/SceneViewNavigation.html). When using the documentation, you can also search for particular words as illustrated on the next figure.

Figure 2-10: Using Unity's manual

THE HIERARCHY VIEW

As indicated by its name, this view lists and displays the name of all objects included in the scene (in alphabetical order by default) along with the type of relationship or hierarchy between them. You may notice that before you add any object to the scene, a camera is already present in the scene so that it can be viewed in the **Game** view through its lenses.

This view offers several advantages when we need to manage all the scene objects quickly and perform organizational changes (e.g., find objects based on their name, duplicate objects, amend objects' names, amend the properties of several objects simultaneously, or change the hierarchy between objects).

For example, on the following figure, we can see that the scene includes four objects: a camera and three cubes.

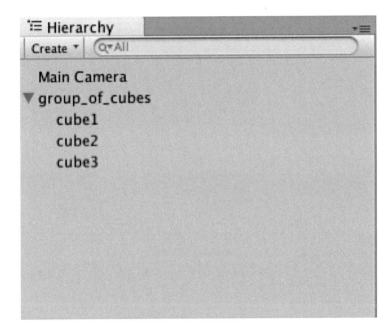

Figure 2-11: Creating a hierarchy between objects

We can also notice that all cubes are grouped under a "folder" (in Unity, this can be created as an empty object in the scene), which means that:

1. All three cubes are children of the object called **group_of_cubes**.

2. The object **group_of_cubes** is the parent of the three cubes.

3. If a transformation (i.e., scale or rotate) is applied to the parent (e.g., group of cubes) it will also be applied to the children (i.e., cube1, cube2, and cube3).

To change the hierarchy of the scene and make some objects children of a particular object, we only need to drag these objects atop the parent object.

THE PROJECT VIEW

This view includes and displays all assets employed in your project (and across scenes), these include: audio files, textures, scripts (e.g., scripts written in JavaScript, C# or Boo), materials, 3D models, scenes, or packages (i.e., zipped resources for Unity). All these assets, once present in the **Project** view, can be shared across scenes.

In other words, if we create a project and then a scene, and import assets for our game, these assets will be available from any other scene within the same project.

As for the **Hierarchy** view, built-in folders and search capabilities are included to ease the management of all your assets.

By default, the **Project** view includes two windows divided vertically (left and right columns). As illustrated on the next figure, the left window includes a folder called assets and a series of "smart" folders (i.e., the content of these folders varies dynamically) called **Favorites**. The right window displays the content of the folder selected on the left-hand side.

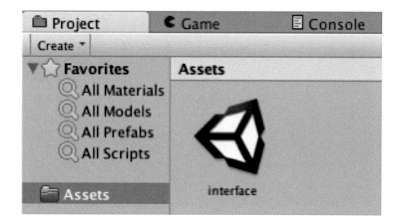

Figure 2-12: The project view

In the previous figure, the content of the folder **Assets** is displayed and consists of the current scene labeled **Interface**. By clicking on any of the smart folders (e.g., **All Materials**, **All Models**, **All Prefabs**, or **All Scripts**) Unity will filter the assets to display only the relevant ones accordingly (e.g., materials, models, prefabs, or scripts). This can speed-up the process of accessing specific assets and can be done (as for many of the functionalities present in Unity) in different ways. For example, you may notice a search window to the left of the **Project** view as illustrated in the next figure.

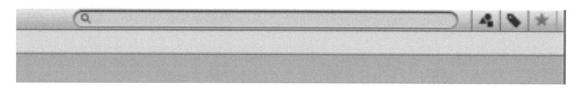

Figure 2-13: Searching for assets in the project

The search window in the **Project** folder can be used to search assets by their name or by their type, as illustrated in the next figure, by clicking on this icon 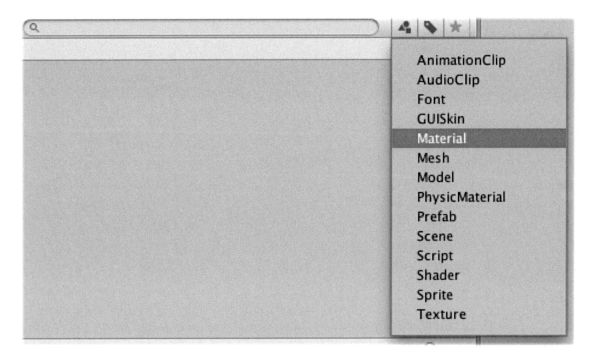 .

Figure 2-14: Filtering through the assets in the project view

As we can see on the previous figure, we have the option to select the type of assets that we are looking for (e.g., **Texture**, **Prefab**, or **Script**). Note that this option can also be specified by typing **t:** followed by the type we are looking for in the search window; for example, by typing **t:material** in the search window, Unity will only display assets of type **Material**.

THE INSPECTOR

This window displays the properties of the object currently selected (i.e., in the **Scene** or **Hierarchy** view) and make it possible to modify the attributes accordingly. All properties are categorized in **Components**.

By default, all objects present in the scene have a name, a default layer (we will look at this aspect later) and a component called **Transform**. However, it is possible to add components to an object using the button **Add Components** or the menu **Component**.

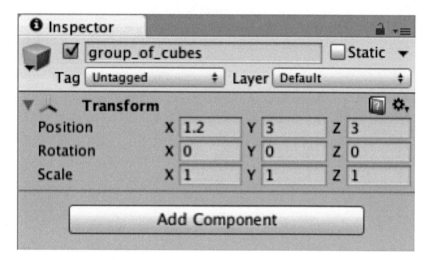

Figure 2-15: The Inspector window

You may also notice a tick box, in the **Inspector** window, to the left of the name of the object, that can be used to temporarily deactivate (and consequently reactivate) the object. This can be useful when you would like to temporarily remove an object from the scene without having to recreate it.

As we will see later, there are many types of components that can be added to an object to enhance it, including physics properties (to enhance how an object will behave realistically following the laws of physics), rendering (to enhance its appearance), or collision (to refine how it will detect collisions with other objects). For example, the default component **Transform** includes the position, rotation and scale of the object selected.

The attributes **tag**, **layer** and **static**, while important, will be covered in later sections.

As we will see later, a scene can be edited and played. However, if we try to modify the attributes of an object while the game is playing, these will not be saved. In other words for modifications to be saved in the scene, they have to be made while the game is stopped (i.e., not played).

THE CONSOLE VIEW

As seen previously, the console window will display messages, from Unity, related to possible errors and warnings in your code that may prevent the game from playing, or messages that you can print through your own code (e.g., for debugging purposes).

THE ASSET STORE WINDOW

This window, which is not displayed by default, connects you to the **Asset Store**, an online repository and market place where you can search for and find assets for your game; some of them are free and some other are premium. This window can be accessed through the main menu (i.e., **Window | Asset Store**) or by using the corresponding shortcut (*CTRL+9*).

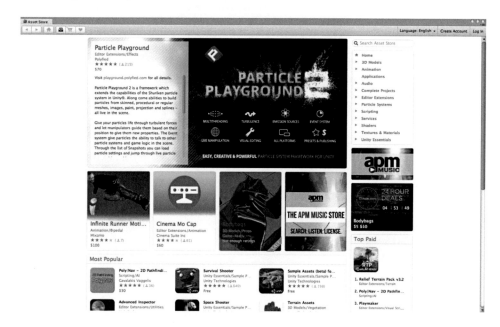

Figure 2-16: The Asset Store view

NAVIGATING THROUGH THE VIKING VILLAGE

While we have looked at the main windows available in Unity, we will now become familiar with navigating through a scene using the project *Viking Village*.

This project is relatively heavy (841MB), so if your broadband connection or the space available on your hard drive are limited, you may, instead of downloading the project, just read through this section, or skip to the next section (level roundup), as many of the shortcuts demonstrated in this section will be covered again later in this book.

You can download this project through the **Asset Store** window as follows:

- Open the **Asset Store** window (*CTRL + 9*).

- Type the text "**Viking village unity essentials**" in the search window (i.e., top-right corner).

- This should return one result.

Viking Village
Unity Essentials/Sampl...
Unity Technologies
★★★★☆ (⊥402)
Free

Figure 2-17: Accessing the Asset Store

- Select the result (i.e., **Viking Village**), this should display the following window:

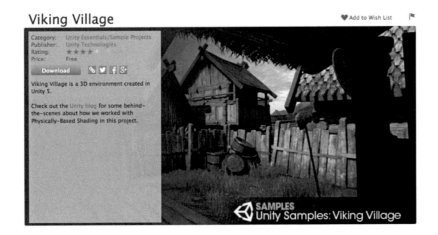

Figure 2-18: Downloading the Viking Village project

- Press the button labeled **Download**. As you press this button, Unity will ask you to login using the email and password provided earlier.

- Once you have entered these details and logged in, we can press the **Download** button again.

- The **Download** button should now be replaced by a progress bar as the project is downloading.

- When the project is downloaded, you can click on the **Import** button.

Figure 2-19: Importing the Viking Village project

- A window labeled **Importing Packages** will appear.

- Click on the button **Import**.

Once you have imported this project, we can now do the following:

- In the **Project** window, look for all scenes available in the project by entering the keywords "**t:scene**" and press the *Return* key; this should display one scene, as described in the next figure.

Figure 2-20: Scenes available in the Viking village project

- We can then double-click on the scene labeled **The_Viking_Village** and it should open accordingly.

  - When the scene is open you may need to zoom-in (i.e., using the mouse wheel or *ALT+CTRL + drag and drop*) within the **Scene** window.

  - Once you have zoomed-in enough, you should see an overview of the Viking village, as illustrated on the next screenshot.

Figure 21: The Viking village from a distance

- You may pan the view to look around by pressing *Q* on the keyboard, then the *Alt* key and by dragging and dropping the mouse within the **Scene** view.

- At this stage we can see that this is a rather complex model, and we will only focus on the player for the time being.

- To do so, let's look at the **Hierarchy** window and enter the keyword **flying** in the search window; this should return two results as follows:

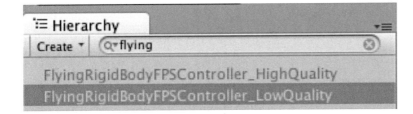

Figure 2-22: Objects' hierarchy in the Viking village scene

- Let's focus the view on the player by double-clicking on the object labeled **FlyingRigidbodyFPSController_LowQuality** in the **Hierarchy** view. The view should now look as follows:

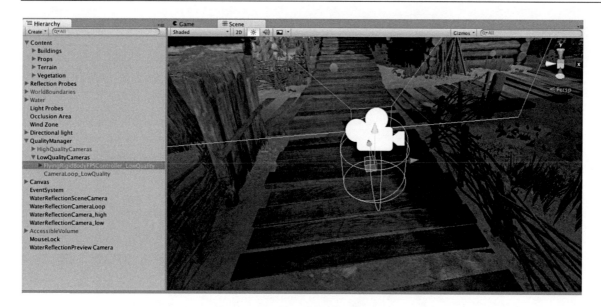

Figure 2-23: Navigating the Viking village scene (focusing on the player)

- The player (or main camera) is now in the center of the view. To see it more clearly, we can zoom-in (*mouse wheel or CTRL + drag and drop*) and look at it from different angles (*ALT + drag and drop*).

Once you feel confortable with these controls (i.e., zooming and rotating around objects), you can navigate through the scene and use other shortcuts as follows:

- Navigate the scene using some of the shortcuts and navigation modes described earlier (e.g., walk or fly).

- Switch from the *WASD* mode to the *Fly Mode* (i.e., Right Mouse Button pressed).

- Select some of the objects present in the scene (i.e., click once or twice on these) and inspect their attributes in the **Inspector** window.

- Try to look at the scene from different axes (i.e., x, y, and z) by clicking on one of the arms or labels of the **Gizmo**.

- Note that if you wish to undo an action (e.g., moving or resizing an object) you can do so by pressing CTRL+Z, as you would do in most software or by selecting **Edit|Undo**.

Once you feel confortable with this navigation, it is time to play the scene by pressing either *CTRL+P* or by clicking on the **Play** button, a black triangle located at the top of the window.

Note that you can maximize the window if need be, so that it occupies the entire screen, either before the game starts or during play. This makes it possible to view your game more clearly.

To maximize the window only when the game/scene is played, you can click on the tab labeled **Maximize on Play** located at the top right corner of the window (this can be cancelled by clicking again on the same tab).

To minimize/maximize the window at any other time, you can simply click on the list located in the top right corner of the window.

- 28 -

LEVEL ROUNDUP

Summary

In this chapter, we have become familiar with the different views and windows available in Unity. We also looked at how to navigate through scenes and how to change the layout of our working environment. In the next chapter, we will harness these skills to be able to create our own 3D environment.

Quiz

It is now time to test your knowledge. Please answer the following questions (e.g., Yes or No). The answers are available on the companion website (http://www.learntocreategames.com/learn-unity-ebook). You don't need to have downloaded the **Viking Village** project to be able to answer these questions.

1. The shortcut to open the **Console** window is CTRL + 1.

2. The shortcut to open the **Project** window is CTRL + 2.

3. The **Viking Village** project was created for Unity 5.

4. The **Console** window can display all the objects included in your scene.

5. The **Project** window can display messages or errors from your code.

6. Once an asset has been downloaded in the scene, it is not available in other scenes within the same project.

7. Once an object has been deactivated (i.e., using the tick box in the **Inspector**) it will be deleted from your project forever.

8. To make some objects children of other objects, you can select the option: **GameObject|Create Child**.

9. Unity is using a right-hand coordinate system.

10. Help on Unity is only available online (i.e., you need to be connected to the Internet to access it).

Checklist

If you can do the following, then you are ready to go to the next chapter:

- Navigate through a scene easily.

- Understand the role of the **Inspector**, **Game**, and **Scene** views.

- Select an object in the hierarchy and zoom-in if need be in the **Scene** view.

- Select an object and look at its properties in the **Inspector** window.

- Answer at least 7 out of 10 of the questions correctly in the quiz.

3

CREATING AND EXPORTING YOUR FIRST SCENE

In this chapter, we will create our first scene, and start to include, combine, and texture basic shapes such as boxes. This chapter explains how to use basic transformations and apply them to objects. It will also explain how to manage and group objects.

After completing this section, you should be able to:

- Create a scene.

- Add basic objects.

- Create and apply colors and textures to objects.

- Add a First- and a Third-Person Controller and explore your scene.

- Group shapes.

- Search for particular objects or assets using shortcuts.

- Export your first scene.

CREATING A NEW PROJECT AND A NEW SCENE

Now that we have covered the main features for the interface, we will create a new project with a simple game where the player has to jump on several boxes without falling. It will be using simple built-in objects and standard assets (i.e., a First-Person Controller) as well as textures and colors for some of these objects.

After completing this section you will be able to:

- Add basic objects to your scene.

- Apply basic texturing and coloring to objects.

- Transform objects (i.e., move, scale and rotate).

- Add a character controller to the scene to be able to walk around the level.

- Add and configure lights.

- Group objects and apply attributes to several objects at a time.

First, let's create a new project and scene:

- Select **File|New Project** and specify a new name and location for this new project.

- Once your new project has been created, select **File|New Scene** to open a new scene.

- This should open a new scene.

- At this stage, we have a blank canvas where we can start to add objects and build our game.

ADDING AND COMBINING SIMPLE BUILT-IN OBJECTS TO YOUR SCENE

As we will see later on, we can create our game environment using a wide range of primitive shapes (e.g., cylinders, spheres, boxes, etc.), lights (e.g., directional lights or point lights), cameras and other built-in assets (e.g., character controllers). Once these objects have been added to the current scene, Unity makes it possible to modify their attributes.

As we open the new scene, you will see that, by default, the scene includes a camera that is called **Main Camera**. This will be the case for any new scene, and we will be able to either delete this camera or modify its properties (e.g., location or orientation) at a later stage.

If you click on this camera in the **Hierarchy** view, you should be able to see a small window labeled **Camera Preview** in the bottom-right corner of the **Scene** view. This preview window represents the scene viewed through the lenses of the camera.

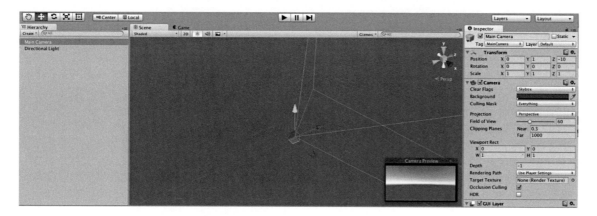

Figure 3-1: Default camera for a new scene

This is how your game will be viewed. At the moment, we can only see a blue screen within the preview (located in the bottom-right corner of the **Scene** view), as no objects or lights have yet been added to the scene. We can also see that the **Inspector** window, that is located to the right of the screen, displays the attributes of this camera. Amongst other things, we see that it is located at the position (**x=0, y=1, z=-10**) and that it has not been rotated yet. Finally, if we look at the **Scene** view, we can see three arrows from the object: one red (along the x-axis), one green (along the y-axis) and the last one blue (along the z-axis).

If you click on the **Game** tab, you will also see a blue screen (as displayed in the camera preview).

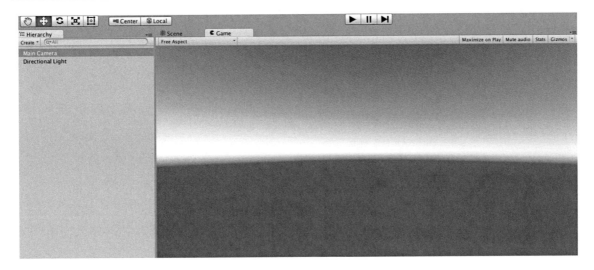

Figure 3-2: Blank game view for a new scene

First let's create a cube that will serve as the ground:

- Switch back to the **Scene** view (i.e., click on the corresponding tab).

- Select: **GameObject|3D Object|Cube**, from the top menu.

- This will create a box that will be, by default, located at **(0,0,0)** with a size of 1. This means that the height, depth, and width of this object are equal to 1.

- Rename the cube **myCube**: to rename the cube, we can (1) select it in the **Hierarchy** window and then press *CTRL+ENTER* simultaneously, (2) select it in the **Hierarchy** window and left-click once on it, or (3) right-click on the object in the **Hierarchy** window and select **Rename** from the contextual menu.

Once you have renamed the cube, we can change some of its properties and see how it affects its appearance. For example:

- In the **Inspector** window, change the **x**, **y**, and **z** scale properties to **2** and see how it affects the size of the cube.

- Change its **y** rotation attributes to **45** (i.e., a rotation around the y-axis expressed in degrees), and see how its orientation has changed. Note that for any of these parameters, you can either change the value in the corresponding text fields, or click on one of the parameters and drag and drop the mouse: this will either increase or decrease the value in the corresponding field. It is usually an easier way to amend an object's attributes.

Once you are comfortable with modifying the transform properties of the cube using the **Inspector**, let's look at other interesting ways to observe the objects and the scene to modify their attributes.

You will notice a tool bar located in the top-left corner of the window, as illustrated on the next figure.

Figure 3-3: Toolbar

This toolbar includes five distinct buttons that are shortcuts to (from left to right) (1) modify the view mode (e.g., pan, or rotate the view), (2) move the object currently selected, (3) rotate the object currently selected, (4) scale the object currently selected, and (5) both move and scale the object currently selected. These five buttons can also be accessed using the key shortcuts *Q*, *W*, *E*, *R* and *T*.

Lets' experiment with the panning tool:

- Select the panning tool from the tool bar (i.e., choose the first icon from the left, or press the key *Q*).

- You should see that the mouse cursor turns into a hand.

- Drag and drop the mouse in the screen view: you should see that you effectively pan the view.

Now, lets' experiment with the **Move** tool:

- Select the **Move** tool from the toolbar or use the corresponding shortcut (*W*).

- You should now see three arrows from the cube. These arrows are handles that you can drag and drop to move the selected object in a particular direction (e.g., along the x-, y- or z-axis).

- As we successively drag the blue, red and green handles, observe how these move your object along the corresponding axes.

Before we look at the three last modes, let's look at a useful widget called a **gizmo**. This widget, as illustrated on the next figure, is located in the top-right corner of the **Scene** view and makes it possible to view the scene from several axes and perspectives.

Figure 3-4: Using the gizmo

Using this gizmo, and by clicking on its **x**, **y**, or **z** arms, we can see the scene from the corresponding axis. Let's experiment with it:

- We can successively click on the **x**, **y**, and **z** arms of the gizmo, and see how the view changes.

- Note that by clicking on the middle of the **gizmo**, we can reset the view to its initial state (i.e., x-axis pointing to the right, y-axis pointing upwards, and z-axis pointing outwards).

- To readjust the view, we can also use the *ALT* key and drag and drop the mouse, so that we can rotate around the object accordingly.

After this short distraction, let's come back to our top-left tool bar and experiment with the three remaining buttons.

Now, lets' experiment with the **Rotation** tool:

- Select the **Rotation** tool from the toolbar (third icon from the left) or use the corresponding shortcut (*E*).

You should now see a combination of green, red, and blue circles around the object. These are handles that you can drag and drop to rotate the object currently selected around a particular axis (e.g., around the x-, y- and z-axis).

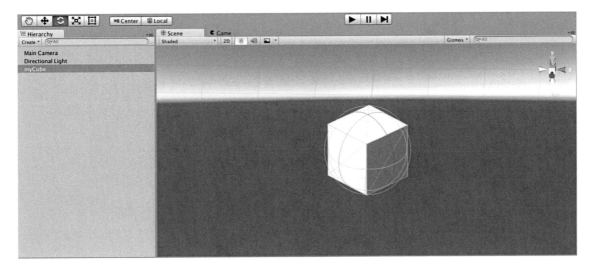

Figure 3-5: Rotating an object

The color of the handle indicates the axis around which the object will be rotated. For example, by dragging and dropping the green handle, we can rotate the object around the y-axis. The same applies to the blue (around the z-axis) and red (around the x-axis) handles.

As we drag these handles, we can see that the values for the corresponding rotation in the **Inspector** also change.

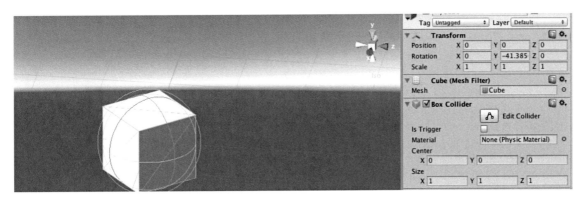

Figure 3-6: Rotating an object around the y-axis

Now, lets' experiment with the **Scale** tool:

- Select the **Scale** tool from the toolbar (fourth icon from the left) or use the corresponding shortcut (*R*).

- You should now see a combination of green, red, and blue lines and handles around the object. These are handles that you can drag and drop to scale the selected object along a particular axis (e.g., along the x-, y- and z-axis).

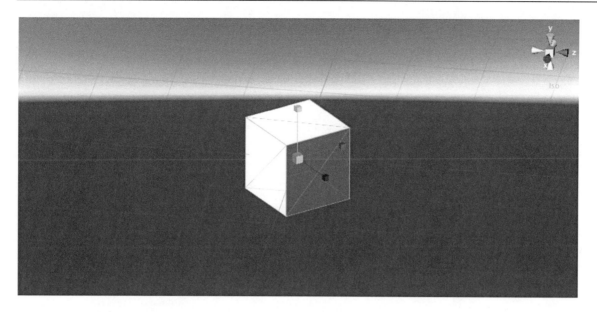

Figure 3-7: Scaling an object

The color of the handle indicates the axis along which the object will be rotated. For example, by dragging and dropping the green handle, we can scale the object along the y-axis. The same applies to the blue (z-axis) and red (x-axis) handles. Also note that by dragging the middle white square, the transformation will be uniform. In other words, the amount of scaling will be the same on all three axes (x-, y, and z-axis).

At this stage, we have performed several transformations on the new cube, and we may want to reset its attributes so that it is the same as when it was initially created. We can do so by using the cogwheel located in the top-right corner of the transform attributes of the cube, as described on the next figure.

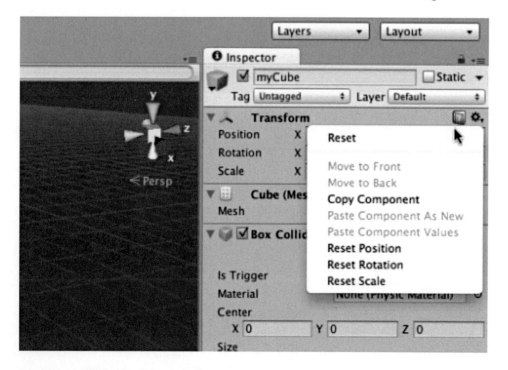

Figure 3-8: Resetting the attributes of an object

The last item on the tool bar is the **Rect** tool. It combines the **Move** and **Scale** tools. Once you have selected the **Rect** tool, you can move the object by dragging and dropping the mouse, or modify the object's width, height, and depth by dragging and dropping the corresponding handles.

For more information and tips on how to use Unity's interface, you can visit: http://docs.unity3d.com/Manual/LearningtheInterface.html

ADDING COLORS AND TEXTURES

At this stage we have a box, a camera, and also a light in our scene. Note that, while the light has been created by default, we could have added light to our scene using the menu: **GameObject | Light | Directional Light**.

- Let's rename the light present in our scene as we have done before (e.g., right-click on the object in the **Hierarchy** view) and rename it **myLight**.

- Once this is done, we will change the orientation and position of the light so that it is above the cube and pointing downwards.

- To do so, we can start by resetting the transform attributes of the light by using the associated cogwheel located at the top-right corner of the **Inspector**.

- As we reset the **Transform** attributes of the light, we see that all its parameters are set to **0**.

- We can now move the light along the **y-axis** so that it is above the cube (e.g., by switching to the **Move** mode).

- We can also rotate the light **90** degrees around the **x-axis** using the **Inspector**.

- If we use the **gizmo** to see the scene along the **x-axis**, we can clearly see that the light is effectively pointing downwards.

Figure 3-9: Rotating the light around the x-axis

Once you are happy with the position of the light, you can rotate around this object using *ALT + drag and drop*, and also look at the scene from the **Game** view.

At this stage, our light is set-up as well as the cube; however, we would like the camera present in our scene to look at the cube from above. We will, accordingly, change the attributes of the camera to implement this feature using the **Inspector**. Note that, we could also add multiple cameras to the scene, and display the image captured by these in different areas of the screen, and we will see this feature later in this book.

- Select the camera in the **Hierarchy** view, as described on the next figure.

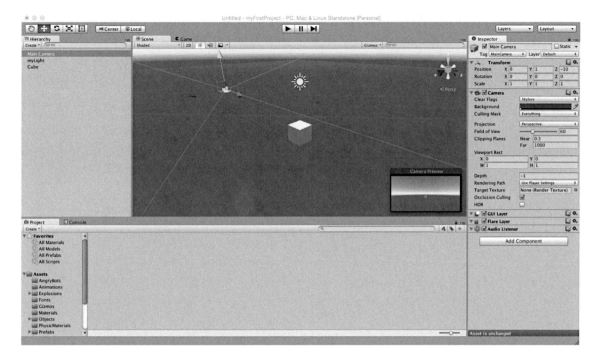

Figure 3-10: Selecting the default camera

So that it is above the cube and pointing downwards, let's change its transform settings as follows:

- **Position: (0, 4, 0)**: we raise the camera four meters above the ground.

- **Rotation: (90, 0, 0)**: we rotate the camera 90 degrees around the x-axis.

Once these changes have been made, the scene should look as illustrated on the next figure. You may notice that, in the **Scene view**, the camera object is symbolized by a camera, and that its field of view is symbolized by what looks like a prism, which encompasses the cube in our scene. This means that the cube is in the field of view of the camera. We can check this in the camera preview window located in the bottom-right corner of the **Scene** view.

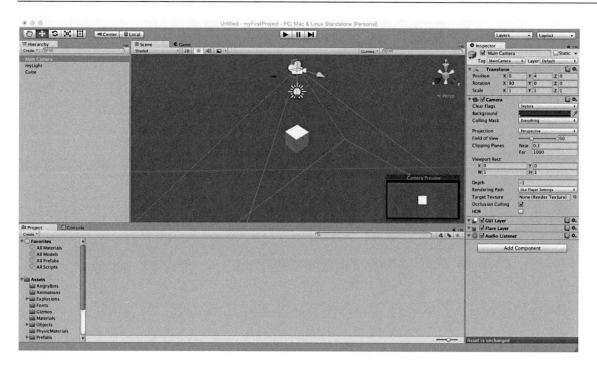

Figure 3-11: Displaying the field of view of the camera

Once the camera has been setup, let's modify the attributes of the light. We will essentially change the color of the light as well as its intensity, so that you can see how these can be amended:

- Select the light in the **Hierarchy** window.

- In the **Inspector**, you may notice a component called **Light**, which includes all the attributes (except for the **Transform** attributes) of the light. Click on the white rectangle to the right of the label **Color**. This will make it possible to modify the color of the light. This may be useful when you need to set the atmosphere in your game and add lights of different colors.

- Once you have clicked on this rectangle, a window labeled **Color** appears. This window is similar to the one used in image manipulation software, such as Gimp or Photoshop, whereby you can pick or define a color based on its RGB code.

For those not familiar with the RGB code, its stands for Red, Green, and Blue and it can be perceived as a palette where we specify the amount of red, green, and blue that will be used to create a new color. In this window, the amount of each color is a number between 0 and 255. Which means that if we use (R=255, G=0, B=0) we will obtain red.

- If we click inside the color window, and choose a color, we can see how the RGB components change accordingly. For the time being, chose a color of your choice, for example a light blue.

- You may also notice an **Alpha attribute (A)** below the amount of blue. This is usually used to specify how transparent a color will be (255 means totally opaque and 0 means totally transparent).

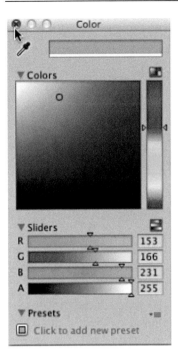

Figure 3-12: Changing the color of the light

Once you have changed the color of the light, you should see that the color of the box will be blue; the same will apply if we switch to the **Game** view.

Creating the ground from a box

So far we have a cube, a camera and a (slightly blue) light in our scene. However, we would like to build a scene where a character walks on the ground and possibly jumps from boxes to boxes or walks up the stairs. The first step in creating this environment will be to set the ground. To create the ground, we can recycle the box that we have already created by modifying both its size and appearance:

- Select the box labeled **myCube.**

- Change its scale properties to **(40, 1, 40)**. This means that we scale it on the x- and z-axes by **40**.

- Rename this box **ground** using the **Hierarchy** window or the **Inspector** (top text field).

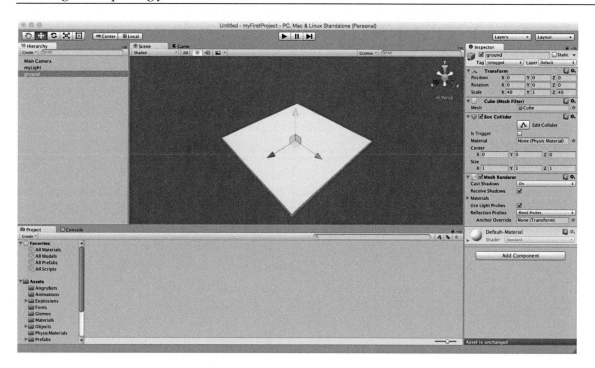

Figure 3-13: Creating the ground from the initial box

Now that we have resized and renamed the ground, it would be great to add some texture to make it look a bit more realistic. For this, we will import a texture asset and apply it to the ground.

You may download a ground texture of your choice or download and use the one provided on the companion website. For this scene, I have saved a texture on my desktop in a folder called *unity_assets*.

In Unity, let's import and apply this texture as follows:

- Select **Asset | Import New Asset...**: this will open a window that makes it possible to import assets in your project. These can be images, audio, or 3D models. Note that assets can be used across scenes, so we only need to import them once in our project, and you can then reuse them in all scene that are part of the same project.

- A window labeled **Import New Asset** should appear, as illustrated on the next figure. You can then select the folder where the images that you have downloaded from the companion website were saved and unzipped, select the relevant texture (i.e., **tile.jpg**), and, finally, click on **Import** to import this asset.

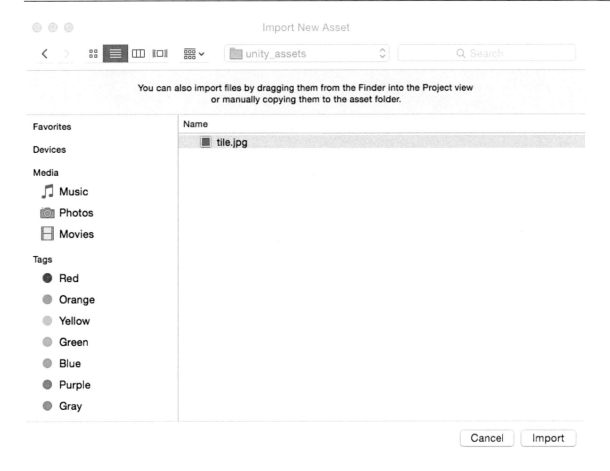

Figure 3-14: Importing an image asset into the project

To see where this asset has been imported, let's click on the **Project** tab:

- As we can see on the next figure, this image has been imported automatically inside the *Assets* folder within the project.

Figure 3-15: Locating the imported asset

- Note that we could create a new Folder (**Create | New Folder**) to organize our assets and move this image to the new folder accordingly.

- To apply this tile to the ground, we just need to drag and drop this image from the **Assets** folder onto the ground object in the **Scene** or the **Hierarchy** view.

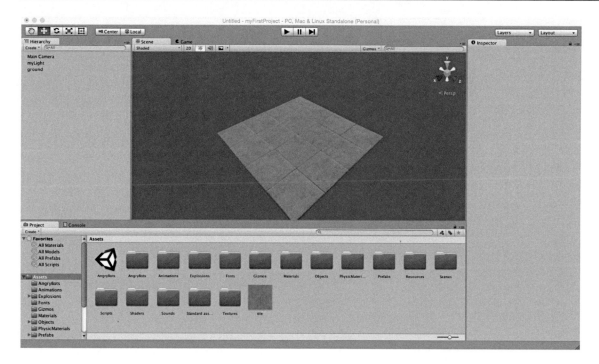

Figure 3-16: Applying a texture to the ground object

As we apply the texture, you may notice that the tiling of the texture, which means the number of times this texture is repeated on the surface of the object, could be improved. At present, based on the gridlines, we see that they are one meter apart.

However, we can change this setting easily using the corresponding material. In other words, whenever a texture is imported and applied to an object, a corresponding material is created, and makes it possible to modify how this texture will be used and perceived (i.e., how it will be rendered). This material is located inside a folder called **Materials**, which is usually in the same folder as the texture. For example, if the texture was imported in the folder **Assets** then the corresponding material would be saved in the folder **Assets|Materials**. Again, if you decided to create a new folder (for example, **Assets|myAssets**) and import this texture in this folder, then the corresponding material would be located in **Assets|myAssets|Materials**.

If we open the folder labeled **Materials**, we can find a material called **tile**. As we click on this material, we can see several of its properties, including **Main Color**, **Tiling** and **Offset**, as illustrated on the next figure.

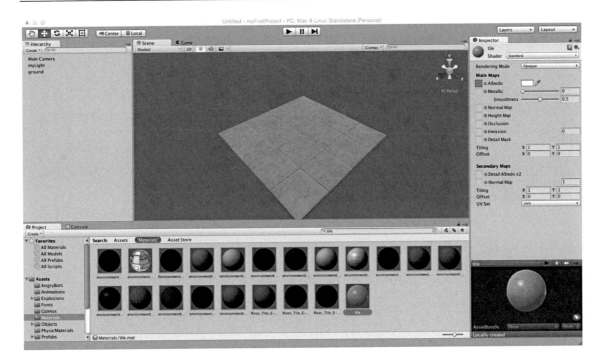

Figure 3-17: Displaying the attributes of a new material

- For now, we will only change the **x** and **y** tiling properties from 0 to **10**. This indicates that the texture will be repeated 10 times on the x- and y-axes.

- After making these modifications, we can zoom-in to look at the ground from a closer range (*ALT + CTRL + drag and drop* or use the mouse wheel).

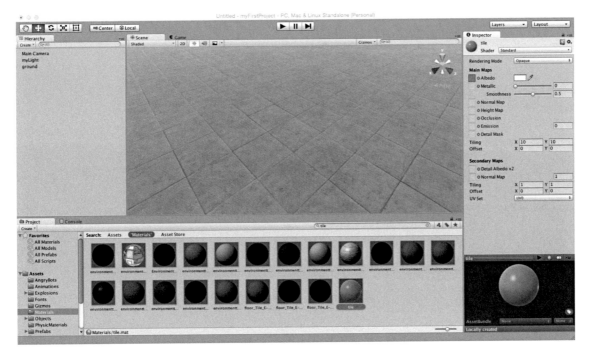

Figure 3-18: Increasing the x and y tiling attributes

You may also notice a sphere, in the bottom-right corner of the screen, which provides an indication of how the texture and material will look like in the game. We can also look at the scene from the game window.

Adding multicolour boxes and stairs

Before we add new objects to the scene, let's modify the attributes of the light slightly, so that it illuminates the scene:

- Select the light labeled **myLight**.
- Change its intensity to **.96** using the **Inspector** window.
- Change its **y** position to **8**.

Once this is done, we will add a succession of boxes using essentially duplications, to speed-up the process:

- Create a new cube (**Game Object | 3D Object | Cube**).

- Rename this cube **redCube** (e.g., in the **Hierarchy** window or in the **Inspector**).

- Change the **y** coordinate (position) of this cube so that it is above the ground; for example, you can use the position **(0, 1, 0)**.

We will now add a color to this cube, using a similar process as for the ground texture:

- In the **Project** window, open the folder **Assets** and then select the folder labeled **Materials**.

- In the **Project** window, you may notice a menu labeled **Create** located in the top-left corner of this **Project** window. This menu makes it possible to create different types of assets for your project, including materials.

- In the **Project** window, select **Create | Material**: this will create a new material asset in this folder.

- Rename this material **redColor** and select it (i.e., click once on it).

- Make sure that this material is selected.

- In the **Inspector** window, click on the white rectangle of the label **Albedo** (or **Main color** in previous version of Unity) to define a color for this material.

- As the color window appears, select a red color.

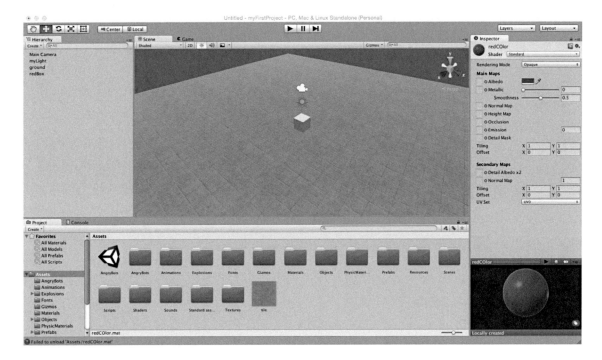

Figure 3-19: Creating a new color for the cube

- Once this is done, we just need to drag and drop this new material onto the cube (in the **Scene** or **Hierarchy** view).

- If we zoom-in to look at the object labeled **redBox** in detail, we can see that the red color has been applied to all sides of the cube.

Now that we have created our first colored cube, we can create similar cubes using successive duplications to speed-up the process:

- In the **Hierarchy** window, select the object labeled **redCube**.

- Duplicate this object: we can right-click on this object and select **Duplicate** from the contextual menu or press *CTRL+D*.

- We can then rename the new cube (i.e., the duplicated object) **greenCube**, and move it along the **x-axis** (i.e., using the red handle).

Figure 3-20: Adding a new cube using duplication

As for the previous section, we will create a new green color:

- In the **Project** window, open the folder **Assets** and select the folder labeled **Materials**.

- Select **Create|Material**: this will create a new **Material** asset in this folder.

- Rename this material **greenColor** and select it (i.e., click once on it).

- Set the color of this material to green.

Once this new **greenColor** material has been created, we can apply it to the second cube and we can check that the color has been effectively applied to all sides of this cube by looking around it (by pressing *ALT* and dragging the mouse).

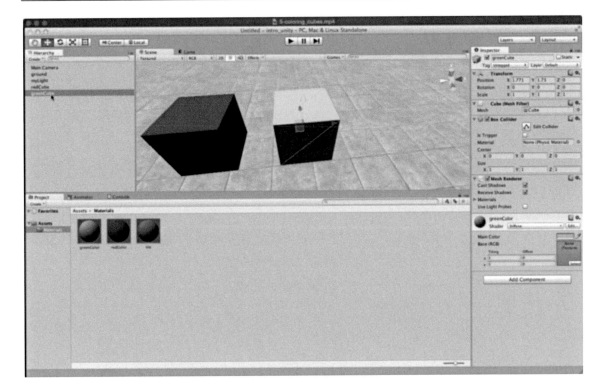

Figure 3-21: Duplicating the initial cube

We can, again, duplicate this green cube, rename this duplicate **greenCube2** and move it along the **x-axis**.

Adding a first-person controller

At this stage, we have a relatively basic scene with a few colored and textured boxes (i.e., for the ground), a light, and a camera. We will, in the next section, import a character controller that we will use to navigate through the scene. This built-in element includes all the necessary features to simulate the movement of a character in a three-dimensional environment (e.g., walking, running, jumping, or looking around)

- Select **Assets | Import Package**: you will see a list of assets that can be imported in your project. These assets are not imported by default, and you can pick and choose which one you will import based on your needs. For now, we will choose the asset called **Characters**.

- Select **Characters** from the list (or **Character Controllers** if you are using an earlier version of Unity).

- After a few seconds, a new window labeled **Importing Packages** will appear.

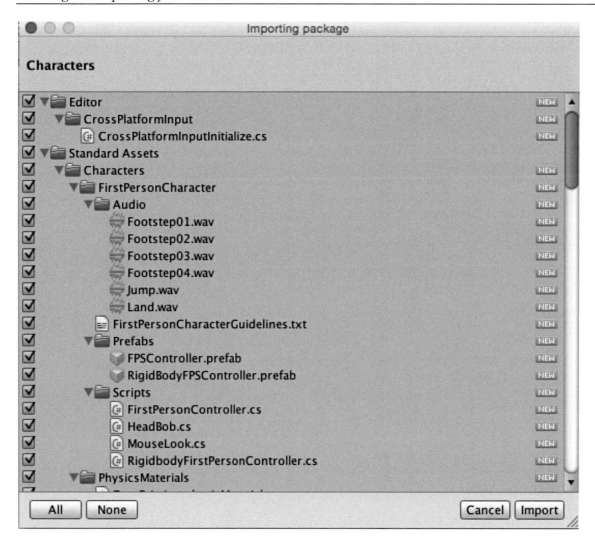

Figure 3-22: Importing character controllers

If you scroll down, you may notice that this package includes a combination of objects, sounds, and scripts. You may also notice tick boxes to the left of these objects. This indicates that you can import selectively. In other words, you can decide which element you wish to import in your project.

For now, as we will import the full package, we will leave all these boxes ticked and click on the button **Import**.

- After a few seconds, the import should be complete.

- These assets, which are imported as part of the package, are usually saved in the folder labeled **Standard Assets > Characters (or Standard Assets > Character Controllers** if you are using a previous version of Unity).

- If you open this folder, we can notice that it includes assets for both the **First-Person Controller** (view from the eyes of the main character) and the **Third-Person Controller** (view from the camera located behind the main character).

Now that we have imported the relevant package, let's use one of the character controllers to navigate through our scene:

- If you are using Unity 5: locate the folder **Assets > Standard Assets > Characters > First PersonCharacter > Prefabs** and drag and drop the icon labeled **FPSController** on to the scene.

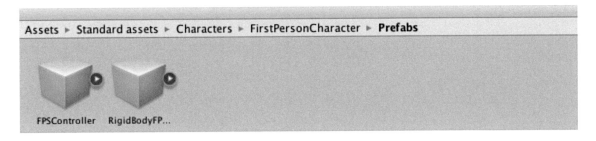

Figure 3-23: Adding the First-Person Controller in Unity 5

If you are using a previous version of Unity (e.g., 4.5): locate the folder **Assets > Standard Assets > Character Controllers** and drag and drop the icon labeled **First-Person Controller** to the scene.

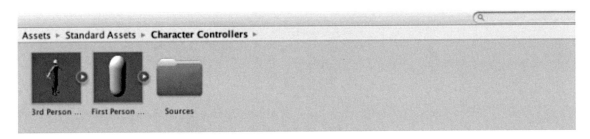

Figure 3-24: Adding a First-Person Controller in Unity 4.x

- Once this is done we can move the FPS controller above the ground in the **Scene** view and check how the game looks like in the **Game** view.

- We will also deactivate the main camera, as we don't need it anymore because the FPS controller includes its own camera. To do so, we just need to select the object labeled **Main Camera** in the **Hierarchy** view, and, using the **Inspector**, deselect the box to the left of the label **Main Camera**.

- After making these modifications, it is time to test the scene by pressing the Play button (the left-most triangle located at the top of the window, as illustrated on the next figure) or alternatively by pressing the shortcut *CTRL+P*.

Figure 25: Buttons to control (play) the scene

- As we play the scene, we can navigate using the arrow keys from the keyboard, we can jump (using the space key), look around using the mouse, or run by pressing the arrow key while also pressing the *SHIFT* key.

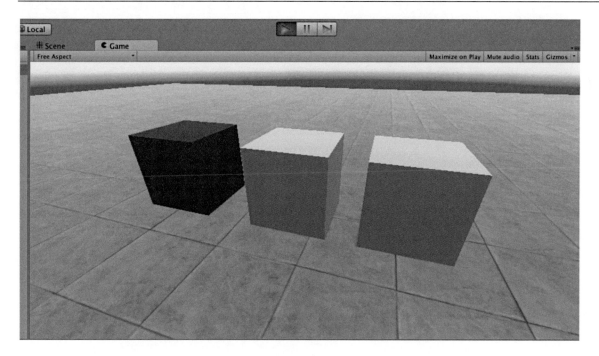

Figure 3-26: Navigating through the scene

Note that you can switch between **Game** and **Scene** views, as the game is playing, to look at the attributes of all objects in the scene. We could also, for example display both views simultaneously by dragging the **Game** view in the lower part of the screen, as illustrated on the next figure.

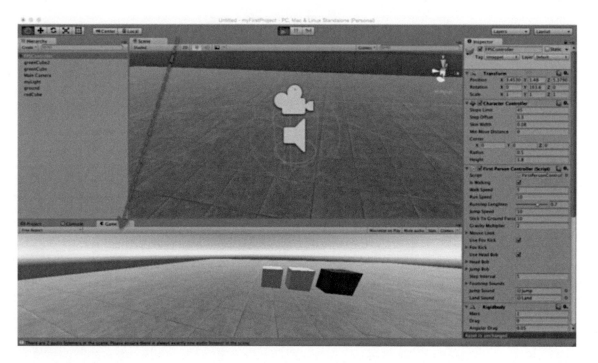

Figure 3-27: Displaying both the scene and the game views simultaneously

Adding a third-person controller

As we have seen in the previous section, Unity offers several types of character controllers to navigate the scene. While we have experimented with the **First-Person Controller**, it would be great to see how the second type (i.e., **Third-Person Controller**) works.

To add a **Third-Person Controller**, the process will be similar to the one we have followed so far, as we will add a corresponding prefab (e.g., a standard asset) to the scene.

If you are using Unity 5: locate the folder **Assets > Standard Assets > Characters > ThirdPersonCharacter > Prefabs** and drag and drop the icon labeled **ThirdPersonController** to the scene.

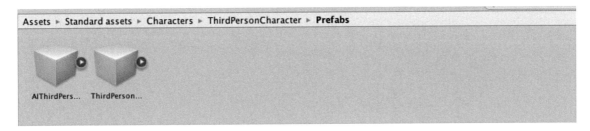

Figure 3-28: Adding the Third-Person Controller in Unity 5

If you are using a previous version of Unity (e.g., 4.5): locate the folder **Assets > Standard Assets > Character Controllers** and drag and drop the icon labeled **3rd Person Controller** to the scene.

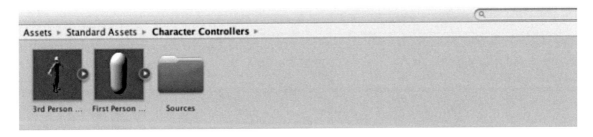

Figure 3-29: Adding a First person Controller in Unity 4.x

- This should create a new object labeled **3rd-Person Controller** in the **Scene** view.

- Once this is done, we can move the **3rd-Person Controller** above the ground in the **Scene** view and check how the game looks like in the **Game** view.

- Before doing so, we will deactivate the **First-Person Controller** that we have included previously, to avoid any confusion between cameras. To do so we just need to select the **First-Person Controller** in the **Hierarchy** view, and, using the **Inspector**, deselect the box to the left of its label.

If you are using Unity 4.x, you are pretty much ready to go and you can play the scene. However, if you are using Unity 5.x, there are a few more things we need to do in order to see our character.

As it is, our new character, while it will be able to move in all directions, will not be displayed onscreen, as there is no camera set up yet it to follow the character. To do so, we need to import a package that includes cameras that have the ability to follow a specific target. In our case, we would like it to follow the character. Thankfully, Unity includes assets that are part of the package called **Camera**, which can do just that. Let's import one of these cameras and use it to follow our character:

- From the top menu, select: **Assets | import Package | Cameras**.

- A new window should appear that describes all the assets (e.g., scripts and objects) included in this package. As we will be importing all of these, click **Import**.

- After a few seconds, the package should be imported. Its content will be located in the folder **Assets > Standard Assets > Cameras**.

- In the **Project** window, locate the folder **Assets > Standard Assets > Cameras > Prefabs** as described on the next figure.

Figure 3-30: Importing camera assets

- As you can see, this folder includes four camera types. For now, we will be using the camera prefab called **MultipurposeCameraRig**. This type of camera can be used to follow a particular target.

Note that while the prefab **FreeLookCameraRig** will follow an object, the **MultipurposeCameraRig**, when used with the player, will ensure that the camera is always rotating so that it adjusts to the player's direction (e.g., behind the player and facing forward).

- Drag and drop the camera prefab labeled **MultipurposeCameraRig** to the **Scene** view.

- Select this object (i.e., the camera) in the **Hierarchy** view, as described in the next figure.

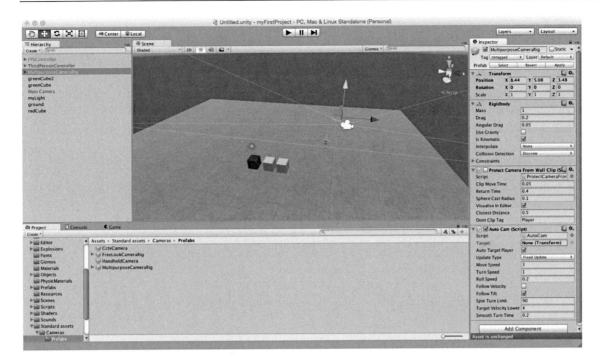

Figure 3-31: Adding the camera to the scene

As you have added the camera to the scene, you may notice, looking at the **Inspector** view, a component called **Auto Cam (Script)**. Within this component, you may see an attribute called **Target** that is currently empty. This field refers to the object that we want to track with the camera. So to track the **Third-Person Controller**, we will need to drag and drop it from the **Hierarchy** view to this field (i.e., **Target**) as illustrated on the next figure.

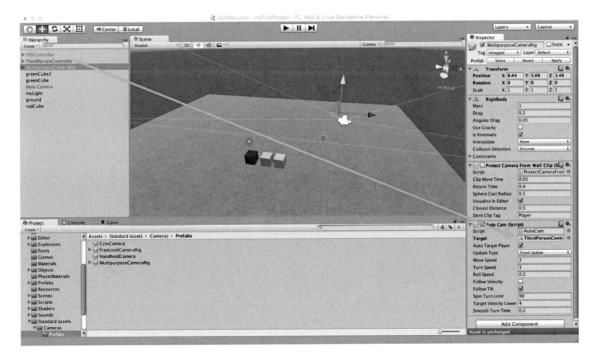

Figure 3-32: Setting the target for the camera

After making these modifications, it is time to test the scene by pressing the Play button or alternatively using the shortcut *CTRL+P (OR APPLE + P* for Mac users*)*. Before you play the scene, just make sure that both the **First-Person Controller** and the **Main Camera** are deactivated.

As we play the scene, we can navigate using the arrow keys from the keyboard, we can jump (using the *SPACE* key), look around using the mouse, or run by pressing the arrow keys on the keyboard, while also pressing the *SHIFT* key.

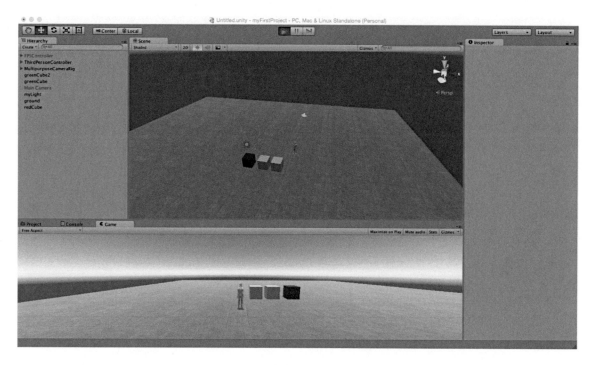

Figure 3-33: Playing the scene with the 3rd Person Controller

CREATING A SIMPLE STAIRCASE

As we have learnt how to create objects, there are a few shortcuts that we could experiment with to speed-up the process of creating a scene. To do so, we will go through a simple example of creating a staircase from boxes:

- Select the object labeled **greenCube.**

- Change its **scale** settings to **(1.5, 0.2, 1).**

- Duplicate it several times.

- Move the duplicates along the x- and y-axes so that they form a staircase.

- Play the scene to experiment with your staircase.

Managing and searching for assets and objects

As we have seen in the first sections of the book, it is possible to look for particular assets and objects in your project and scene using search windows and keywords. Let's use these for our project and start with the **Hierarchy** window:

- If you look at the **Hierarchy** window, you may notice a search window located in its top-right corner. It can be used to look for items in your scene based on their names.

- If we type the word **cube** in this search field, it will list all the objects with a name that includes the word **cube.** You may also notice that in this case, as illustrated on the next figure, other objects do not appear in the scene anymore.

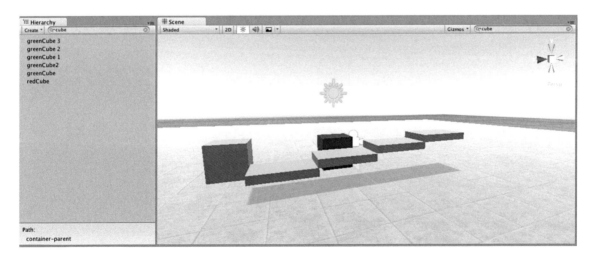

Figure 3-34: Searching in the hierarchy (cubes)

In a similar way, if we type the word **green** for example, it will list all the objects which names include the word **green.** You may also notice, as illustrated on the next figure, that other objects in the scene do not appear anymore in the **Scene** view (they are greyed-out).

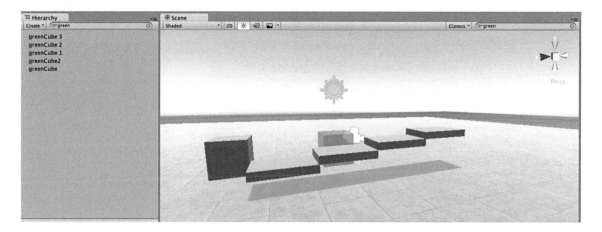

Figure 3-35: Searching in the hierarchy (green objects)

Let's see how we can perform searches in the **Project** window:

- If we click on the **Project** window, you may notice a search window located in its top-right corner.

- After typing the word **color**, Unity will show all assets with a name that includes this word; in our case, it includes both the materials **redColor** and **greenColor**.

Figure 3-36: Searching for assets (color)

- Using the word **tile** for the search, Unity will show all assets with a name that includes this word; in our case, it includes both the texture and the material labeled **tile**.

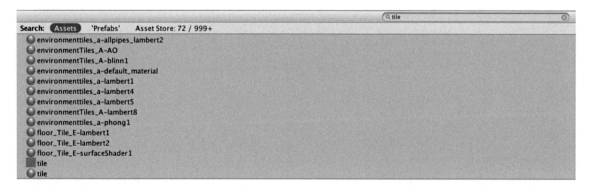

Figure 3-37: Searching for assets (tile)

- After typing the keywords **t:material**, Unity will show all assets of type material in the project; these include the three **Material** assets **tile**, **greenColor** and **redColor** that we have created previously.

- Finally, after typing the keywords **t:texture**, Unity will show all assets of type **Texture** in the project; these include the texture labeled **tile** that we have imported in our project.

Another interesting feature is the ability to group objects. As it is, for example, we have built a staircase; however we would like to move all the stairs as a whole, rather than each of these individually. It is possible to group all of these by creating a folder, which, in the **Hierarchy** view, is often used or referred as an empty object. Let's see how:

- Select: **Game Object|Create Empty.**

- Rename this object **container-parent.**

- Next, select all the cubes that make-up the stairs (click on each object while pressing the *CTRL* key or the *SHIFT* key).

- Once they are all selected (except from the **container-parent** object), drag all of them on the object **container-parent.**

- As you do, you will see a black triangle to the left of the object **container-parent** in the **Hierarchy** view and all previous objects listed under this object.

- If we select the object **container-parent** in the **Hierarchy** view and use the **Move** tool, we can see that by moving this object, all the children are also moved accordingly.

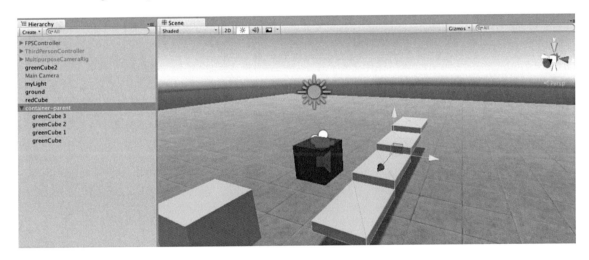

Figure 3-38: Grouping objects

SAVING THE SCENE

At this stage, we can save the project (**File|Save Project**) and also save our scene:

- Select **File|Save Scene As...**

- Choose a name for your scene, for example **scene2.**

- Press **Save.**

By default, the scenes are saved in the current project. You can see all scenes included in your project by looking at the **Assets** folder or by using the search field in the **Project** window with the keywords **t:scene** (to display all the scene part of the current project).

Whenever you are saving a file in Unity or importing assets, these files will be saved in the active folder (the folder that is currently selected). So, to save a file in a particular folder, you will need to check that this folder has been selected in the **Project** window beforehand.

EXPORTING OUR SCENE TO A WEB BROWSER

While we have created a very basic scene, it would be great to export it and see how it will look in a browser.

- Select: **File | Build Settings:** this window helps to specify the settings for the game we would like to export, including the scene(s) to be used and the format of the output.

- For now, we will only include the current scene.

- In the section **Scene In Build**, select and delete any item present in the list. This is so that not all scenes in the project are included in the build. In other words, we are being selective as to what scene should be included to possibly reduce the size of the files created for the build.

- Once the list is clear, click the button **Add Current Scene** to add the current scene to the build, and select **Web Player** in the **Platform** section.

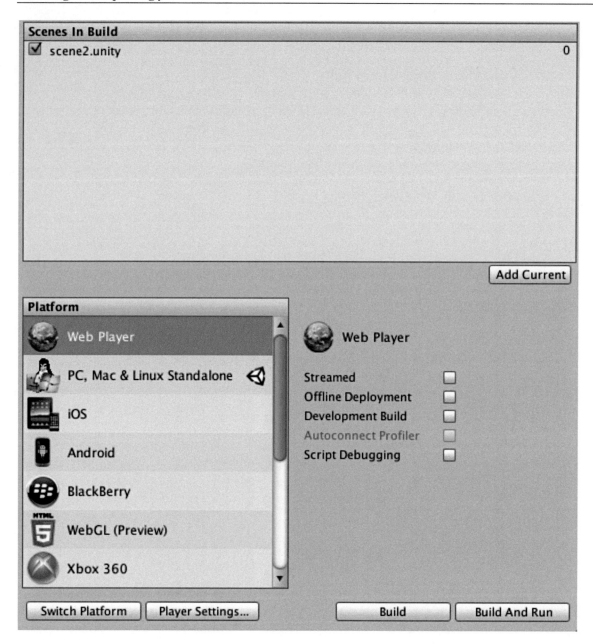

Figure 3-39: Build settings

- Leave all the other options as default and click on the button labeled **Build and Run.**

- A new window will appear asking for the name of the build. You can type **myFirstGame.** This will create a folder and a Unity file with the same name within your project folder by default. This being said, you can choose to export the game to other locations of your choice.

Once the build is complete, your default browser will be launched and the game should appear.

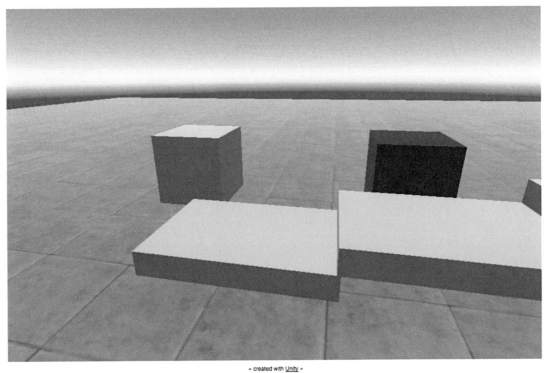

Figure 3-40: Viewing your game in a browser

Please note that at this moment in time, and although Web export works in Unity, it may no be supported by Chrome, as the support for the NPAPI plugin, which is used when displaying a Unity scene in a browser, is being progressively dropped by several browsers (for security reasons).

If you are using Chrome, the following solution is temporarily available until Chrome 45 (late 2015):

- In the address bar at the top of the screen, type **chrome://flags/#enable-npapi**

- In the next window, click the link that says **Enable** under the **Enable NPAPI** flag.

- In the bottom-left corner of the page, click the **Relaunch Now** button.

LEVEL ROUNDUP

SUMMARY

In this chapter, we have learned about several core features in Unity. We became more confortable with the interface and learned how and why to use the different views. We also learned how to add and transform built-in assets, including cubes, lights, and cameras. We also looked into how to modify the appearances of each box by importing or creating materials. Building on this knowledge, we created a simple level with a staircase and ground, and added two types of controllers so that we could navigate through the scene. We looked at different ways to manage the assets included in our project by grouping them (using empty objects) and searching them with corresponding search windows and keywords. Finally, we have learned how to export our scene so that it can be viewed in a web browser.

Quiz

It is now time to test your knowledge. Please answer the following questions (e.g., Yes or No). The answers are available on the companion website (http://www.learntocreategames.com/learn-unity-ebook).

1. In Unity, all files and scenes are always saved in the folder **Assets**.

2. When importing a package, any of its items can be imported selectively.

3. For each texture used in Unity, a corresponding material is created automatically.

4. The **RGB** code is used for colors.

5. The key *Q* is the shortcut for the **Move** tool.

6. The key *R* is the shortcut for the **Scale** tool.

7. The **Rect** tool can be used to select all objects in a particular area.

8. In Unity 5, the **Third-Person Controller** includes a built-in camera that follows its movement by default.

9. The syntax "**t:material**" in the **Project**'s search window will return objects for which the label includes the letter **t** or the word **material**.

10. It is possible to see the content of both the **Game** view and the **Scene** view at the same time.

Checklist

You can move to the next chapter if you can do the following:

*   Add a combination of built-in objects to your scene.

*   Add a color or a texture to your objects in the scene.

*   Include built-in packages (assets) that you can use to walk across the scene (i.e., first- or third-person controllers) or add camera

effects (e.g., to follow a target).

- Manage and search for assets in your projects using relevant search windows and keywords.

- Group objects (using empty objects), and create a parent object, so that transformations are applied to all of the children (rather than individual transformations).

- Change the layout of your project's windows to suit your workflow.

Challenge 1

Now that you have managed to complete this chapter and that you have gathered interesting skills, let's put these to the test. This particular challenge will get you to become super comfortable with shortcuts.

Create a robot that does not have to be animated, as follows:

- Use built-in shapes (e.g., spheres, boxes, or cylinders).

- Combine these shapes to create the different parts of the robot.

- Group these shapes for the arms and legs, for example.

- Use duplication to speed-up your workflow (e.g., duplicate the left leg or the left arm).

Challenge 2

Create a platform game where the player needs to jump between boxes (platforms) to reach the end of the level; you can do as follows:

- Create a new scene.

- Add, move, and resize boxes.

- Add textures to these boxes.

- Add a first- or third-person controller.

- Test the game.

- Import the script called **resetPlayer** from the resource folder downloaded from the companion website and drag and drop this script on top of the **First-** or **Third-Person Controller**. This script will ensure that your character controller is reset to its initial position if it misses a box and falls. You don't need any scripting skills for this, but, if you are curious, you can look at how the script is designed.

- Test the game and check that whenever the player falls, it is reset to its initial position.

4

TRANSFORMING BUILT-IN OBJECTS TO CREATE AN INDOOR SCENE

This chapter helps you to create an indoor scene using basic shapes and textures. Following the previous chapter, you will use your skills to modify shapes (e.g., move, scale, rotate). You will also learn to configure lights, and textures (e.g., tiling).

After completing this section, you should be able to:

- Be more confortable with manipulating and transforming objects.

- Understand how a texture can be tiled over an object.

- Configure the intensity of a light.

- Understand how to set-up ambient light.

- Understand how to use the **Rect** tool to speed-up the design process.

THE PLAN

When you start creating a game, and although there are many resources available out there, you may just want to create a quick mockup to test the key features before you can (or hire someone who can) create a more polished level. Although you may have a 3D modeling background, many beginners, who may not have this skill, may need to be able to create their level fast with basic shapes. This chapter will help you to do just that: to create a functional level with relatively simple shapes. For our first level, we will create a scene with the following features:

- A maze (i.e., indoor scene) with lights, textured walls, a ground and a ceiling.

- Safe areas.

- Dangerous areas where the player could be exposed or trapped.

To create this environment, we will be going through the following process:

- Use a predefined map of the maze in the form of an image.
- Use this map to add objects to our scene.
- Remove this map.
- Add textures to all objects in the scene.

Without a predefined map, it may be difficult to know where to add the different objects that will make up your scene. You can, of course, use coordinates (place the object based on a list of predefined coordinates); however, using a map, you can visually assess whether each object to be included is at the right location, as you expected. In our case, we will be texturing the floor with the map, then add objects atop the floor, based on the outline of the maze, and then replace this texture (i.e., the outline) with tiles, once all the objects have been added.

The layout of our level is illustrated on the next figure; it essentially consists of a succession of corridors.

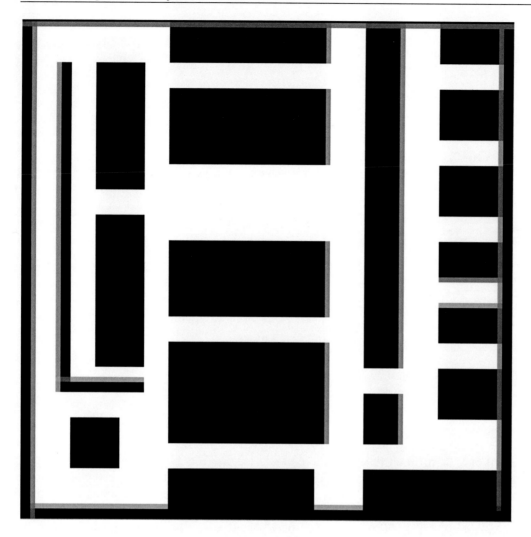

Figure 4-1: Outline of the maze

As you can see, this is a rather simple black and white image that was created in *Photoshop*. It consists of a white background (which symbolizes empty spaces) and black rectangles of different sizes. You can create a map of your choice very easily using *Paint* or *Gimp* also. The idea of this map is to simplify the creation of the maze in Unity by specifying, even roughly, the location of the different parts of the maze, so that we don't have to guess where to add objects, but instead follow a guide and our initial plan. For the purpose of this chapter, this image was created using Photoshop. Its size is 100 by 100 pixels, and, if you are using *Photoshop*, you can also activate the grid lines every 5 pixels (subdivisions every second pixel).

CREATING A SCENE AND IMPORTING NECESSARY ASSETS

Before we start to create this environment, we will create a new scene and a corresponding folder where all the assets that we need will be stored. We will also import some of the textures required for this level.

First, let's create a new scene:

- Assuming that the project we have created in the previous chapter is open (otherwise, you can open it using **File | Open Project**), create a new scene (**File | New Scene**) and save it as **chapter4** (or any other name of your choice). Once this is done, we have a blank scene with no objects in the **Hierarchy** or **Scene** view, except from a camera and the light.

We can now create a folder for our scene. While this is not compulsory, it helps to organize our project and to include and save all relevant assets used for this scene in a particular folder.

- In the **Project** window, click on the folder labeled **Assets**, and then select **Create | Folder** from the menu located in the top-left corner. This will create a new folder labeled **New Folder** within the folder **Assets**. Note that we could also have right-clicked on the folder **Assets** and selected the option **Create** from the contextual menu to perform the same action.

- Let's rename this folder **chapter4** (or any other name that you would like to use instead): right-click on the folder, select the option **Rename** from the contextual menu, and enter the new name for this folder (e.g., **chapter4**).

At this stage, you have already downloaded the resources for this book from the companion website. For this chapter we will need to import the images *bricks.jpg, ceiling.jpg, and gameMap.jpg*. We can import these textures in at least two ways.

Using drag-and-drop:

- Open the folder **Assets | chapter4** in Unity.

- Locate the folder, that you have downloaded and unzipped from the companion website, in your file system.

- Drag-and-drop the images *bricks.jpg, ceiling.jpg, and gameMap.jpg* to the folder **chapter4** in Unity.

Using the **Import** option:

- Select the folder **chapter4** in Unity.

- Select **Assets | Import New Asset** from the top menu.

- A new window called **Import New Asset** will appear.

- Locate the folder where you have saved the images on your system.

- Select the file to import and click **Import**.

- Repeat the previous step for each of the images to be imported.

DEFINING THE OUTLINE OF THE MAZE

At this stage, we are ready to start creating our maze. First, we will create a cube that will be used for the ground:

- Create a new cube (select **Game Object|3D Object|Cube**).

- Using the **Inspector**, ensure that the position of this cube is **(0, 0, 0)**.

- Rename this cube **ground** using the **Hierarchy** window (*CTRL + Enter*) or the **Inspector**.

- Using the **Inspector**, change the scale properties of this object to **(100, 1, 100)** so that it is scaled-up on the **x**- and **z-axes**.

We will now apply a texture to this object:

- To make it easier to see the changes, we can change the view to look at the object from the y-axis. This can be done, as previously, using the **Gizmo** located in the top-right corner, by clicking on its **y-axis**.

- Once this is done, we can navigate to the folder that includes the texture that we have just imported, including the image for the ground, using the **Project** window (i.e., **Assets|chapter4**). Once you have located this folder, as well as the texture that we need to use for the outline (**gameMap.jpg**), drag and drop this texture from the **Project** window to the object labeled **ground** in the **Scene** (or the **Hierarchy**); this will, as we have seen in the previous section, apply the texture to the **ground** object, as described on the next figure.

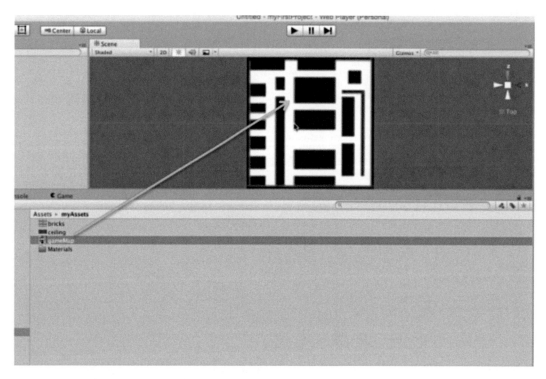

Figure 4-2: Applying a new texture to the ground

As for previously, you will notice that a folder called **Materials** was created within the folder **chapter4**, and that it contains a new material labeled **gameMap**. If you remember, this file will define how our texture will be expressed and rendered.

If we click on this material (i.e., the material **gameMap** that is located in the folder **Material**), and look at the **Inspector** to check its properties, you will see that its tiling properties are **(1, 1)**, which means that the texture is tiled only once on both the x- and the y-axis, and that's exactly what we need because the texture is supposed to represent the entire level. This is the reason why we will leave this default option as it is.

ADDING WALLS USING SIMPLE TRANSFORMATIONS

Now that the ground has been defined, it is time to create walls and other rooms, based on cubes; let's create our first room:

- Create a new cube and rename it **room1**.

- Position this cube just above the ground (e.g., **Position: y = 1**).

- You may also change the view (if you have not already done so) to a top view using the **gizmo**, so that you can view the scene from the **y-axis**.

We will now perform a series of transformations on this cube so that it fits one of the black rectangles on the ground texture:

- Select the cube **room1**.

- Select the **Rect** tool using the shortcut R or by selecting this tool in the corresponding toolbar as illustrated on the next figure.

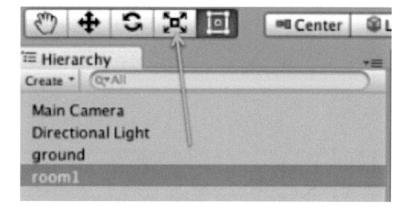

Figure 4-3: Selecting the Rect tool

When this tool has been selected, zoom-in on the object **room1** (e.g., double-click on this object in the **Hierarchy**), you should see blue handles appearing at each corner of the cube, as described on the next figure.

Figure 4-4: Using the Rect tool on a cube

We can now resize the cube by dragging and dropping one of its handles so that it matches the designated black rectangle on the outline (i.e., the map defined by the texture on the ground).

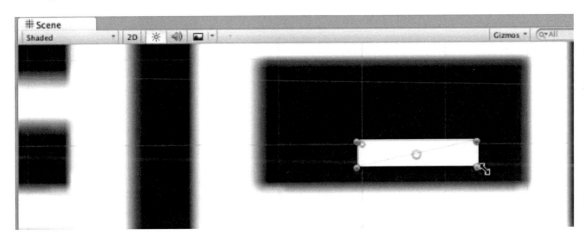

Figure 4-5: Matching the ground texture

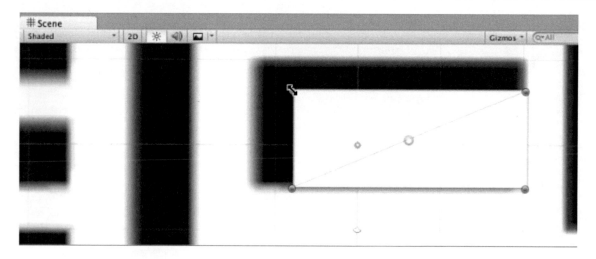

Figure 4-6: Completing the first room

After successive iterations, we have managed to create the first room by matching the texture on the ground, as illustrated on the next figure.

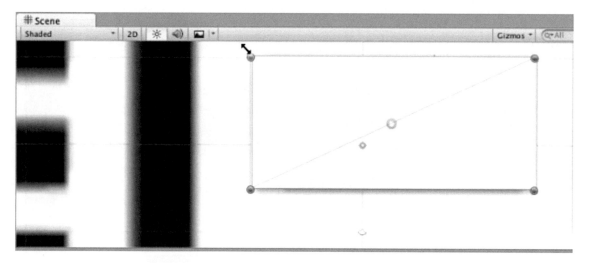

Figure 4-7: Completing the first room (continued)

At this stage, we have managed to rescale the room along the x- and z-axes; however, we also need to modify its height. We would like the ceiling to be 2.5 meters high; however, its current y position, which is usually calculated from its centre, is 0; this means that, effectively, if we set a **y** scale factor of **2.5**, the actual distance between the ground and its center will be 1.25 meters. This means that only half of the cube will be above the ground; so we need to move this cube upwards. Let's apply these changes in the **Inspector** window:

- Check that the object **room1** is selected.

- In the **Inspector** window, modify the **y** position attribute to **2.5**.

- In the **Inspector** window, modify the **y** scale attribute to **5.0**.

Once this is done, we can apply a texture to this room:

- Navigate to the folder **Assets | chapter4** (or any folder where you have stored the pictures for this chapter).

- Drag and drop the texture **bricks** located in this folder to the object **room1**; this will also create a corresponding material in the folder labeled **Materials** (**Assets | chapter4 | Materials**).

- Change the tiling of this texture by modifying the **tiling** properties of the **brick** material (located in the **Materials** folder) to (**x=10, y=2**). This setting is arbitrary and you may use different scaling properties based on the texture that you have applied. To make sure that the tiling looks realistic, you may first zoom-in on the object, and then modify the tiling properties, so that you can observe and apply the **x** or **y scaling** values that work best for you.

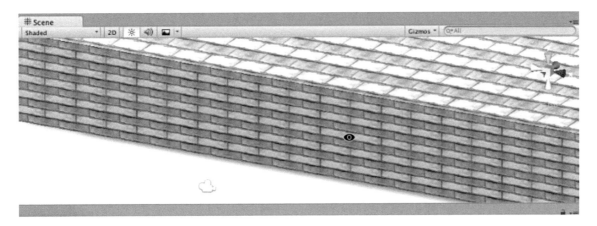

Figure 4-8: Adding a texture to the room

Once you are happy with the look of the room, we can duplicate this room and resize it to create another room:

- Duplicate the object **room1** in the **Hierarchy** view and call the new object **room2**.

- Move the duplicate near another black rectangle on the outline, and resize it so that it matches the area perfectly (i.e., at this stage, only the x and z **position** and **scale** attributes need to be modified). You can use the **Move** tool to move the object, and the **Rect** tool to resize it.

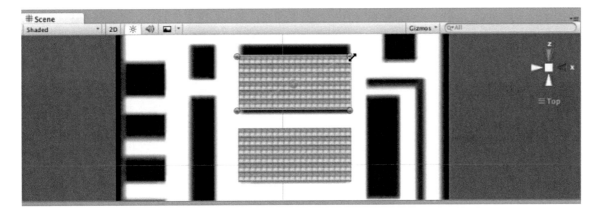

Figure 4-9: Duplicating the initial room

You can repeat this process to complete the entire maze.

CREATING THE EXTERNAL WALLS

Once you have created all the different rooms, the maze should look as described in the following figure.

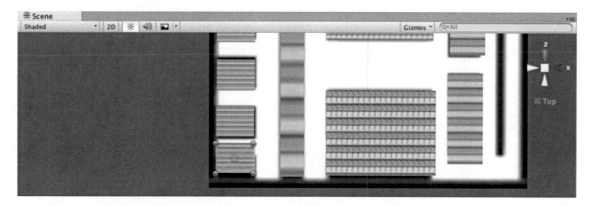

Figure 4-10: The maze almost completed (without external walls)

You may notice that the texture that we used for the rooms differs depending on the room it was applied to. This is because the tiling was based on the length of the initial room; we can leave this option as it is for now; however, if you wanted to increase the aesthetics of some of the rooms, you could define specific materials for some of them so that the tiling is set accordingly (since the tiling is linked to the material, a change in the **tiling** settings involves changing or creating a new material).

So at this stage, our maze is almost complete, it only needs at least three elements: external walls, a roof, and some light.

So let's create the external walls.

To create the external walls, we can start by creating a duplicate of any other wall, and then resizing this duplicate. For example, we could, as illustrated in the next screenshots:

- Duplicate the box located in the bottom-left corner of the screen (*CTRL + D*).

- Rename this duplicate.

- Resize the duplicate to obtain one of the external walls (using both the **Rect** and **Move** tools).

- Check that the wall matches the boundary defined by the outline image.

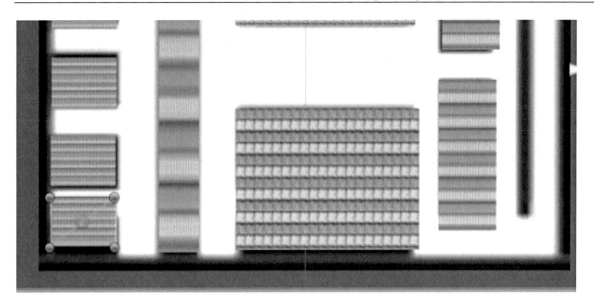

Figure 4-11: Duplicating an existing object

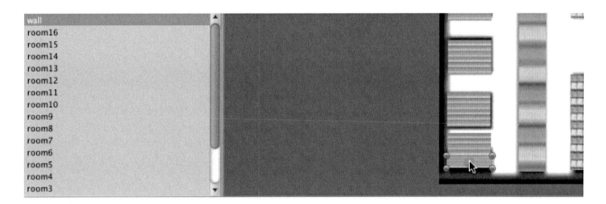

Figure 4-12: Creating the first external wall - part 1

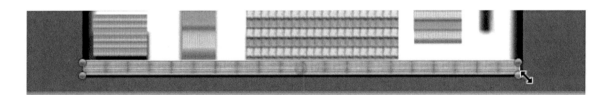

Figure 4-13: Creating the first external wall - part 2

Figure 4-14: Creating the first external wall - part 3

As you can see, the process is rather easy, and we can repeat it to create the three other external walls:

- Duplicate the external wall three times.

- Transform and move the duplicates to their corresponding location on the outline.

ADDING A FIRST-PERSON CONTROLLER TO NAVIGATE THROUGH THE SCENE

At this stage, we have managed to create the floor, several rooms, and external walls for our maze, and it would be great to be able to navigate through the maze. If you remember the first chapters of the book, we used **Character Controllers** to navigate through our platform game. We will do the exact same here, and add a **Character Controller** to the scene so that we can walk through the maze and see how it will appear to the player. Because the scene that you are now creating is part of the same project as the one using platforms, the character controllers **prefabs** are still available in the **Standard Assets** section. In other words, we will not need to reimport this package. So let's do the following:

- In the **Project** window, navigate to the folder **Standard Assets|Characters|FirstPersonCharacter|Prefabs**.

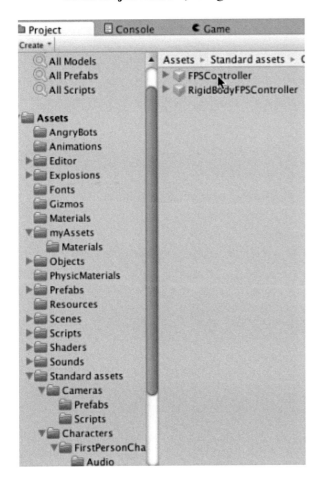

Figure 4-15: Adding a first-person controller

- Drag and drop the prefab (blue box) with the label **FPSController** to the scene.

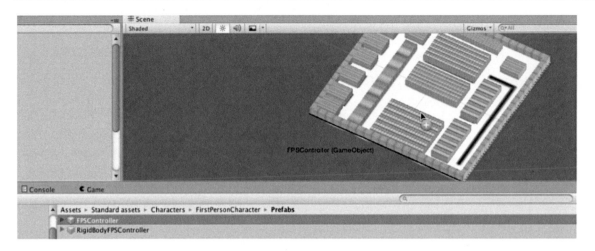

Figure 4-16: Adding a first-person controller (continued)

- Once the **FPSController** has been added, a new object labeled **FPSController** should appear in the **Hierarchy** window.

- Double-click on this item in the **Hierarchy** window to zoom-in on this object.

- In the **Scene** view, move the **FPSController** so that it is slightly above the ground; as you will see on the next screenshot, my position for the **FPSController** is **(-2.3, 1.37, -9.25)**; however, these may vary depending on how you have implemented the maze.

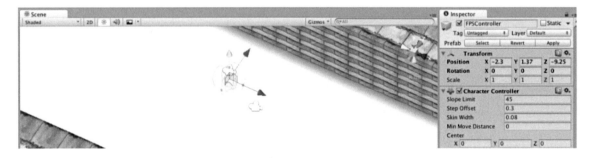

Figure 4-17: Adjusting the first-person controller

At this stage, if you click on the **Game** tab, you may see a glimpse of the maze viewed through the lenses of the **FPSController**, as illustrated on the next figure.

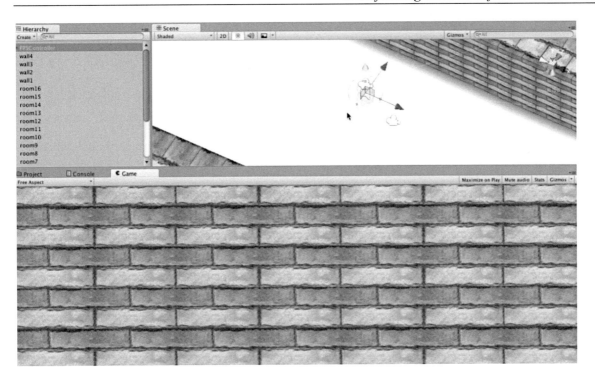

Figure 4-18: Seeing the view from the FPSController

CHANGING THE TEXTURE OF THE GROUND (REMOVING THE IMAGE TEMPLATE)

At this stage, our level is pretty much ready to be viewed, except for the ground. If you remember, the texture used for the ground has been, until now, a template with white and black boxes that indicated where to add cubes that defined rooms. Because we have completed the layout for the maze, we don't need this texture anymore. We can, instead, use a more realistic texture for the ground, such as the tile **texture** that we had initially applied to the ground in the previous chapter. So let's make this change:

- In the **Scene** view (or the **Hierarchy** view), click once on the object labeled **ground** so that we can see its properties in the **Inspector** window.

- Once the **ground** has been selected, look at the **Inspector** window and locate the component called **Mesh Renderer.**

- Within this component, in the section called **Material**, click (on the small circle) to the right of the texture **gameMap** so that we can edit and change the texture allocated to this object.

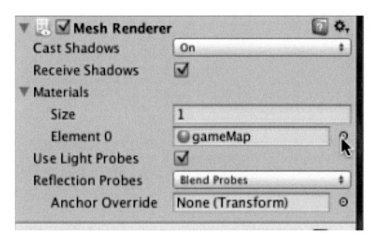

Figure 4-19: Changing the texture for the ground

After clicking on this icon, a new window labeled **Select Material** will appear, so that you can select another material for the ground.

At the top of this window, enter the text *tile* in the search field. This should filter the textures in the project to only display those for which the name includes the word **tile**. You can then select the **tile** texture from the results of the search.

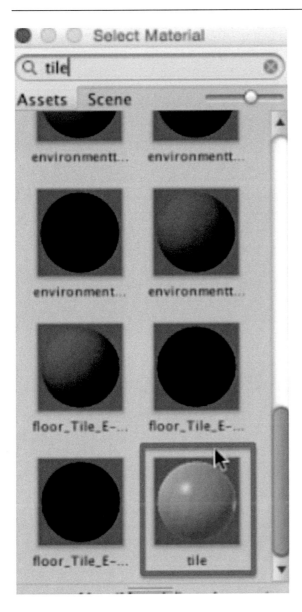

Figure 4-20: Selecting a new texture

- Once you have clicked on this texture, the **Inspector** window should now list this material for the object **ground** as highlighted on the next figure.

Figure 4-21: Texture set for the ground

- You will also see that the texture of the **ground** has changed in the **Game** and **Scene** views.

After this change, it is now time to play our scene and navigate around it:

- Press the **Play** button (or *CTRL + P*).

- Navigate through the scene.

- It should look as described on the next figure.

Figure 4-22: Scene with a ground texture

ADDING A CEILING TO THE MAZE

Once you have checked that the environment looks as expected, we can stop playing the scene. At this stage, the level is functional; however, as mentioned earlier, it would be great to include a roof. This can be done easily by copying the ground, moving it up, and changing the associated texture. We will use the same techniques as before (by using the **Move** tool and changing textures in the **Inspector**):

- Using the **Hierarchy** window, search for the object *ground*.

- Once you have located this object, duplicate it (*CTR + D* or right-click + duplicate).

- Rename the duplicate **ceiling**.

- In the scene view, and using the **Move** tool, move up the object labeled **ceiling** so that it is slightly above the other walls, for example to the position **(0, 5, 0)**.

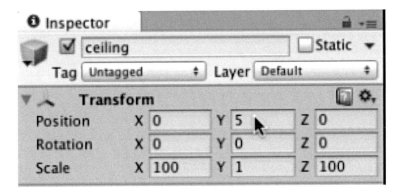

Figure 4-23: Position attributes for the ground

Once this is done, we just need to apply a texture to this ceiling:

- Import the texture called ceiling from the folder downloaded from the companion website and save it in a folder of your choice within Unity (e.g., **Assets|chapter4**).

- In Unity, in the **Project** window, go to the folder where you have saved this texture.

- Then drag and drop this texture onto the **ceiling** object in the **Hierarchy** or **Scene** view.

Figure 4-24: Applying a texture to the ceiling (before changing the tiling attributes)

As you drag and drop it on the ceiling, you will notice that the texture is tiled only once on the surface of this object; so, as previously, we will need to change the tiling properties of the material associated to the texture we have just used.

Remember, whenever a new texture is applied to an object, a new material is created in the folder called **Materials**. This material will dictate how the texture is to be displayed (e.g., including how many times it is to be tiled).

- You may also notice, in the **Project** window, that a new folder called **Materials**, has been created (or updated, if the texture has been saved in the same location as the previous textures) in the folder where this texture was saved.

- Open this folder (i.e., **Assets|chapter4|Materials**).

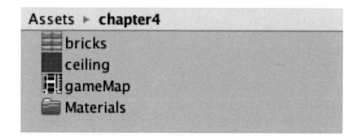

Figure 4-25: Selecting the material for the texture ceiling

- Within this folder, select (i.e., click on) the material called **ceiling**.

- Once the object is selected, look at the **Inspector** window, and change the tiling properties of this object to **(x=20; y=20)**.

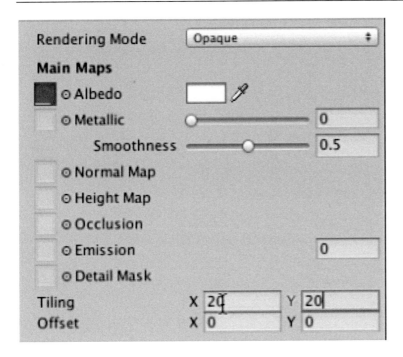

Figure 4-26: Changing the tiling properties of the current material

When looking back at the **Scene** view, you can now see that the tiling of the texture for the ceiling has changed, as illustrated on the next screenshot.

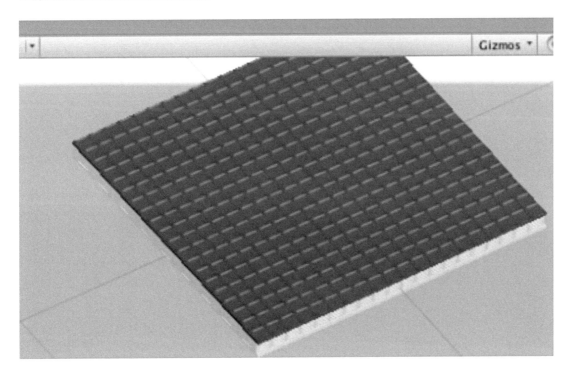

Figure 4-27: Ceiling with a new tiling (20 by 20)

We can now play our scene to see how this new texture looks like.

Figure 4-28: Ceiling with a new tiling

As you navigate through the maze, we may well discover areas that are bright, where the light from outside the maze shines through, indicating that the ceiling is probably not covering the maze properly. But you can always readjust its size and position at a later stage to ensure that this is fixed.

Figure 4-29: Bright areas in the maze (light from outside)

You may be wondering why you can still see the walls if the environment is perfectly closed. We will see this in more detail later on, but in a nutshell: your scene has default attributes, and some of these are related to the amount of ambient light in the scene. By default, even if no lights have been added to the scene, there will be some ambient light. This, of course, can be modified, and we will do so in the next section.

ADDING LIGHT TO THE SCENE

Once you have amended the maze, we will start adding light to it, to create some dark and bright areas. In your game, this could be used to conceal areas or to highlight rooms or corridors where the player should go. There are many different types of lights in Unity, and for the time being, we will just use **Point Lights** to simulate the light created from a bulb, or a torch light, that shines from a specific point in all directions.

Because the ceiling is now the top-most object when looking at the scene from the y-axis, we can temporarily deactivate it so that it is easier to add and move objects within the maze. To do so:

- Select the object labeled **ceiling** in the **Scene** (or the **Hierarchy**) view.

- In the **Inspector** window, deactivate this object (by unchecking the box located in the top-left corner of the **Inspector** window).

Once this is done, we can start to add lights to the scene:

- From the **GameObject** menu, select **Light|Point Light**.

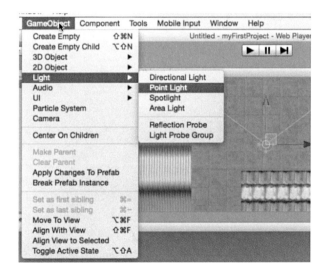

Figure 4-30: Adding a Point Light to the scene

- This will create a **Point Light**.

If the object that you had selected prior to creating the lights was, for example, the **FPSController**, the light will be created at the same location. In other words, new objects are created at the same position as the object selected before the new object is created.

- You should now see a new object labeled **Point Light** in the **Hierarchy** as well as a new light in the **Scene** view.

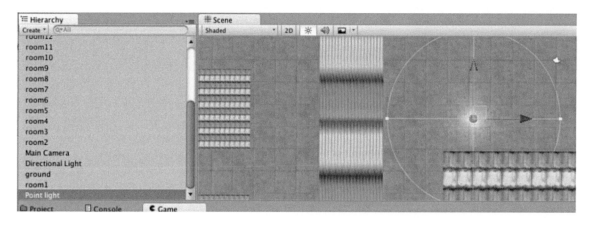

Figure 4-31: Adding a point light

- Select this new object in the **Hierarchy** view, and look at the **Inspector** window to see the properties of this light.

- If you look at the component called **Light**, you will see several properties that will make it possible to customize the light, including **Range**, **Color**, or **Intensity**.

- For now, we will change the **Range** to **20** (i.e., 20 meters) and the **Intensity** to **1.63**.

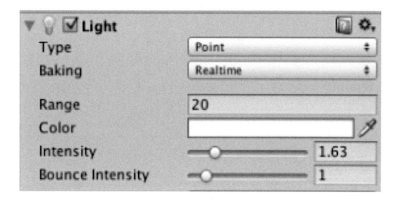

Figure 4-32: Modifying the light properties

Once these changes have been made, let's deactivate the external light:

- Locate the object labeled **Directional Light** in the scene.

- In the **Inspector** window, deactivate this object (by unchecking the box located in the top-left corner of the **Inspector** window).

- You should now see that the scene is much darker, as illustrated on the next screenshot.

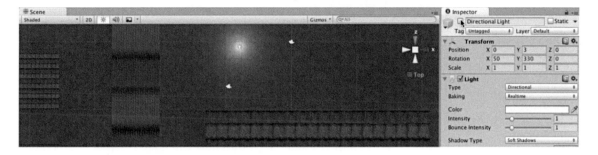

Figure 4-33: Scene without the external light

- You can also reactivate the ceiling (i.e., select the **ceiling** and check the box located in the top-left corner of the **Inspector** window) and play the scene that should now look like the following figure.

Figure 4-34: Navigating the scene without external light

After checking the scene, we can reproduce the last steps to include more lights, by either duplicating and moving the **Point Light** we have created or by using the menu **GameObject | Light | Point Light**, as follows:

- Temporarily deactivate the **ceiling**: this will make it easier to move the lights.

- Duplicate the **Point Light** that you have created previously several times to locations of your choice, making sure that most corridors are lit up properly.

- Modify the settings for each light and amend their **Range**, **Intensity** or **Color** to create special effects of your choice.

- Reactivate the ceiling, play the scene and see how these look like.

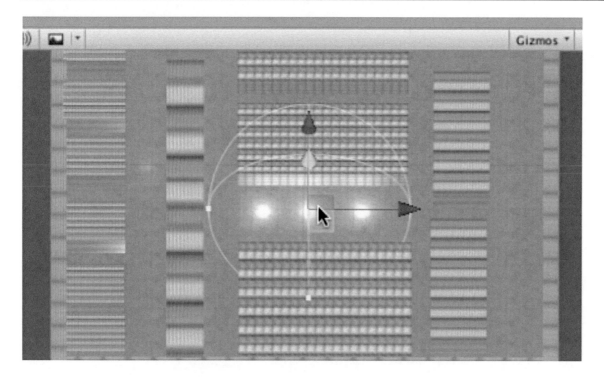

Figure 4-35: Including additional point lights

As you can see on the next picture, the point lights can be used to highlight points of interest.

Figure 4-36: Navigating the new scene (with more point lights)

Last but not least, we need to make sure that areas with no light are completely dark, regardless of the ambient light; so let's modify the project settings accordingly.

- Open the menu: **Window|Lighting**. This window will deal with most of the light settings for our project.

Figure 4-37: Accessing the lighting properties

- The **Lighting** window should then open. As you will see, it includes several tabs and sections. For now, click on the tab called **Scene.**

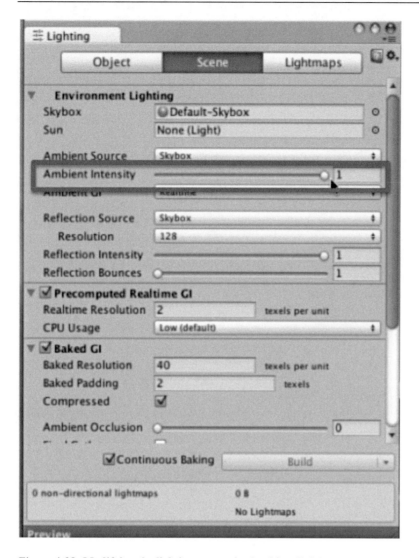

Figure 4-38: Modifying the lighting properties (ambient light)

- In the section called **Environment Lighting**, reduce the option **Ambient Intensity** to 0; as you do, look at the scene view and observe how the maze progressively becomes darker and darker.

- Once this is done, you can close the **Lighting** window and play the scene again.

LEVEL ROUNDUP

Summary

In this chapter, we have become more comfortable with the creation of an indoor environment and we learned how to create a maze from built-in objects such as boxes, point lights, or cameras. We used the skills acquired in the previous section to transform objects and create a fully functional level.

Quiz

It is now time to test your knowledge. Please answer the following questions (e.g., Yes or No). The answers are available on the companion website (http://www.learntocreategames.com/learn-unity-ebook).

1. The shortcut to move an object is Q.

2. The shortcut to rotate an object is R.

3. The **Ambient Lighting** can be modified using the menu **Windows|Lights**.

4. **Intensity** is an attribute of both **Ambient** and **Point lights**.

5. If no lights have been added to the scene, the scene will be completely dark.

6. New objects are always created at the position **(0,0,0)**.

7. **Tiling** is one of the attributes of all textures used in a scene.

8. Once a texture has been applied to an object it cannot be replace later.

9. A tiling property of (1,1) means that the picture will be repeated once on both the x- and the y-axis.

10. The shortcut *CTRL +D* is used to delete an object.

Checklist

You can move to the next chapter if you can do the following:

*   Apply a template to create a scene.

*   Duplicate objects.

*   Move and transform objects to create a maze.

*   Change the tiling property of a texture.

*   Add lights to a scene.

*   Modify the intensity and color of the default ambient light for a scene.

Challenge 1

For this particular challenge, you will need to create a new maze, based on a new template as follows:

*   Import the texture **gameMap2** from the folder that you have downloaded from the companion site.

*   Apply the same techniques as before to recreate the maze based on this outline.

*   Add lights at locations of your choice.

Challenge 2

For this challenge, you will need to create your own outline using the image manipulation tool of your choice and then apply it to create a totally new maze of your own design!

You could proceed as follows:

- Create a new image with a size of 100 pixels by 100 pixels.

- Set the background to white.

- Set the foreground colour to black.

- Create the maze using a brush of size 1.

- Save your image in the **png** or **jpg** format.

- Import this image into Unity.

- Create a new scene.

- Use this new template to create your own new maze.

5

CREATING AN OUTDOOR SCENE WITH UNITY'S BUILT-IN TERRAIN GENERATOR

In this chapter, we will start to use Unity's built-in asset packages to create an outdoor scene and navigate through it using different types of vehicles.

After completing this section, you should be able to:

- Create a realistic landscape from a template.

- Create a terrain and modify it to produce hills and valleys.

- Simulate water.

- Add and control built-in vehicles such as cars and aircrafts.

- Add and customize cameras to obtain top-down views of the environment.

THE PLAN

For this chapter, we will create an island and we will also add two vehicles to it (a car and a plane), so that you can navigate through and above the island easily. So the plan is pretty simple:

- Import a template that we will use to draw the outline of the environment.

- Create a terrain based on this template.

- Paint over the template using Unity's built-in **Terrain** tools.

- Create hills and valleys.

- Add trees and other types of foliage.

- Add buildings based on boxes.

- Add and drive a car in this environment.

- Add and pilot an airplane.

- Customize the cameras so that the vehicles are always in sight.

The next screenshot is a preview of what you will have accomplished after completing this chapter.

Figure 5-1: Preview of the car on the beach

Figure 5-2: Preview of the island with trees

Figure 5-3: Preview of the island with a building and hills in the background

As you can see, you will be able to create a very simple, yet realistic environment.

THE ISLAND OUTLINE

For this level, we will be creating an island. As per the previous chapter, we will be using an image created in Photoshop to define its outline and main features.

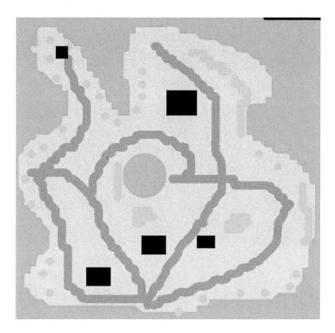

Figure 5-4: The outline of the island

As you can see, this is a rather coarse outline, but it gives an idea of the shape of the island. You may notice the following:

- Water surrounding the island in blue.

- Sand for most of the island.

- Brown patches to highlight paths.

- Green dots to identify the location of trees.

- Black rectangles to indicate the position of buildings.

- A lake in the middle (blue circle).

This image is 500 pixels by 500 pixels and it will be mapped so that 1 pixel roughly equates to 1 meter in Unity. If you want to create your own outline, you can do so easily using these settings. The map does not have to be extremely detailed because, as you will see later, we will be able to paint over it and also remove (i.e., erase) some of its elements. What is important for now is that you have an outline that you can use directly in Unity.

DOWNLOADING NECESSARY MATERIAL

All material necessary for this chapter is included in the resource pack that you have downloaded at the start of the book; if you have not done so, you can find this material on the companion website on the following link:

http://www.learntocreategames/learn-unity-ebook/

IMPORTING NECESSARY ASSETS

At this stage, we are ready to start with our island. If you remember well, we will be adding trees and a terrain that will mimic the shape of the island; for this purpose, we need to import specific packages to be able to complete these tasks. These packages include terrain assets and water assets. The terrain assets include all necessary textures and objects needed to build and amend a terrain, while the water assets make it possible to create realistic water effects. Let's import these assets:

- In Unity, select: **Assets | Import Package | Environment**.

- A new window labeled **Importing Package**, should appear. This will take a few seconds or minutes, depending on the speed of your computer. As for other importing windows, it will list all the items that you can import within this package.

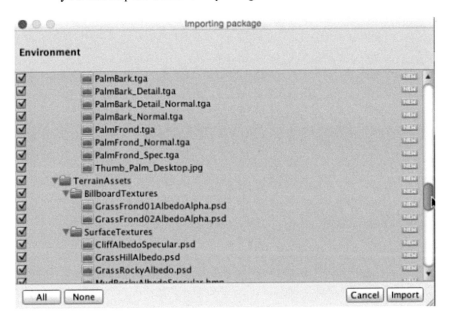

Figure 5-5: Importing the Environment package

- We will be importing all assets in this package, so we can leave all the boxes ticked and click on the button **Import**.

- Once the import is complete, you will notice an additional folder labeled **Environment** within the folder **Standard Assets**, as illustrated on the next figure.

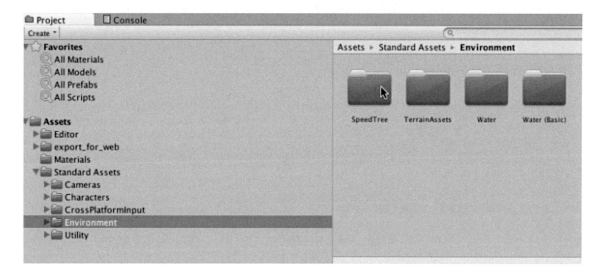

Figure 5-6: Locating the Environment package in the Assets folder

As you can see, this folder includes several other folders with assets related to terrains, water, or trees.

At this stage we have all the necessary assets to create our island, except from the outline map. So let's import it:

- Switch to your file system (e.g., explorer or Finder).

- Locate the folder where you have downloaded the resource pack at the start of this book.

- Select the file labeled **gameMapOutdoors.png**.

- Drag and drop this file inside the **Project** window as illustrated in the next figure.

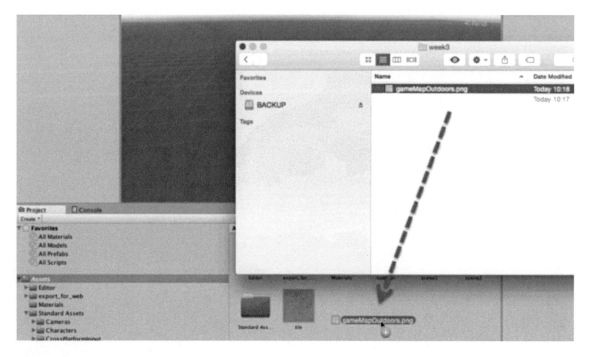

Figure 5-7: Importing the outline file

CREATING THE OUTLINE OF THE ISLAND

At this stage, we have most of the assets that we require to start. So let's create the terrain:

- Create a new terrain by selecting: **GameObject | 3D Object | Terrain**. While we used boxes to create floors before, terrains behave like real terrains in that they can be raised or lowered; they include trees and other features to create realistic outdoor scenes.

- This should create a new object labeled **Terrain** in the **Hierarchy** view.

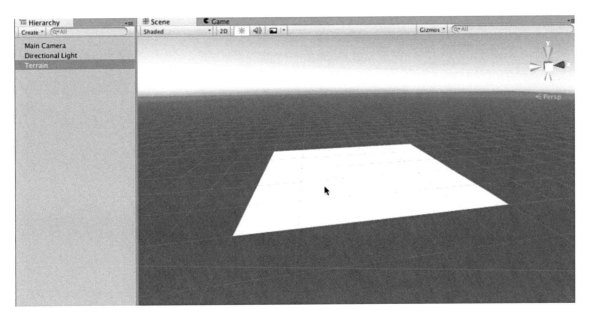

Figure 5-8: Adding a new terrain to the scene

Next, we will paint this terrain:

- Select the **Terrain** in the **Hierarchy** window.

- Check that the size of the terrain is 500 by 500: click on the terrain **Settings** button, as highlighted on the next figure.

Figure 5-9: Selecting the terrain's settings

- Scroll down to the section called **Resolution** and check that the terrain's **Width** and **Length** are set to 500. This is important so that the image that we have created for the outline can match the terrain perfectly.

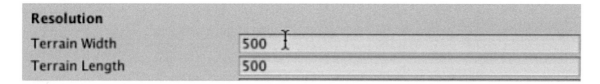

Figure 5-10: Checking the terrain's width and height

- In the **Inspector** window, click on the **Paint** tool for the terrain, as highlighted on the next figure.

Figure 5-11: Selecting the Paint tool

- Then, click on the button labeled **Edit Texture**, and select **Add Texture** from the contextual menu: this will make it possible to edit the texture to be applied on the terrain.

- A new window called **Add Terrain Texture** will appear.

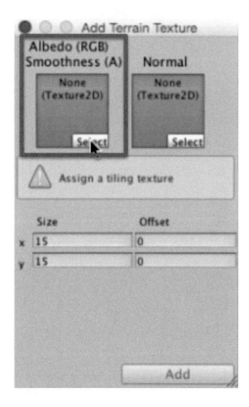

Figure 5-12: Selecting a texture

- Click on the **Select** button, to the left, for the **Albedo (RGB)**.

- A new window will appear in which you can search for and select the texture **gameMapOutdoors**.

- Type the keyword **gamem** in the search field, and then click on the texture **gameMapOutdoors** once it appears in the search results, as described on the next figure.

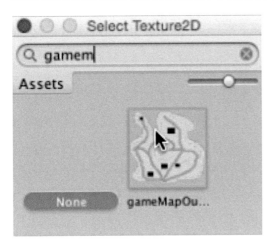

Figure 5-13: Selecting the gameMapOutdoors texture

- Once this is done, you will be back to the previous window; it will show that the texture has been selected.

- Set the size of the texture to match the size of the terrain: set the **x** and **y** values to 500. This will match exactly the size of the terrain.

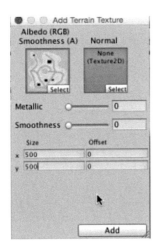

Figure 5-14: Setting the size of the texture

- Click on the button **Add.**

- Using the **Paint** tool (i.e., the tool currently selected), click once on the terrain in the **Scene** view to apply this outline to the terrain.

At this stage, the texture has been applied and the **Scene** view should look like the following figure.

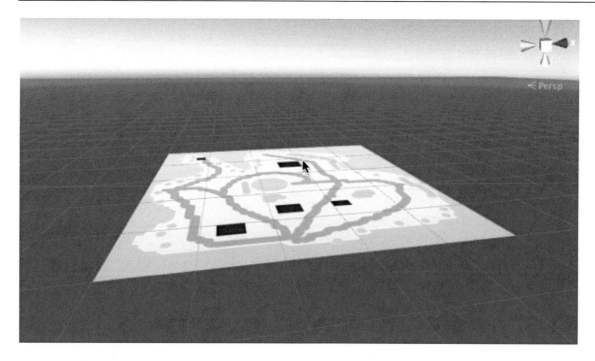

Figure 5-15: Overview of the island with a texture

GIVING DEPTH TO THE TERRAIN

So far, we have managed to apply the outline of the island, and that's great. It is now time to add some depth to the terrain.

- Make sure that the terrain is selected.

- Select the **Paint Height** tool from the **Inspector** window, as highlighted on the next figure.

Figure 5-16: Selecting the Paint Height tool

- Within the same tab, in the **Settings** section, set the **Height** to 5.

- Then press the button labeled **Flatten**.

Figure 5-17: Flattening the terrain

Flattening the terrain will raise the entire island and ensure that we can carve or raise portions of it. This step is important to be able to create any hills or valleys on the island. If you are unsuccessful in raising the terrain later on, this could be due to missing this step.

At this stage we are ready to carve into the terrain; one of the first things we will do is to carve the outline where there is water, as the water level should be below the ground level.

- Let's switch to a more convenient view so that we can see the scene from the **y-axis**: locate the **Gizmo** in the **Scene** view and click on its **y-axis**; this should switch the view accordingly.

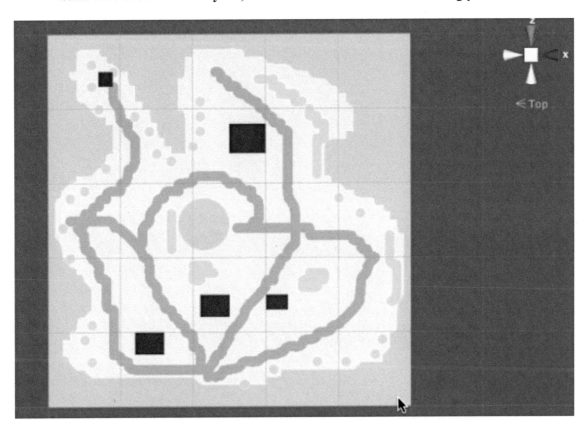

Figure 5-18: The island viewed from the y-axis

- You might as well zoom-in on the bottom right corner of the terrain using successively the mouse wheel and the **Pan** tool (*Press Q + drag and drop*).

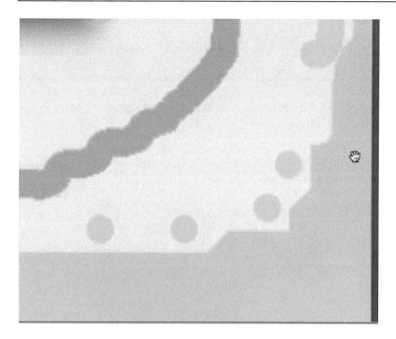

Figure 5-19: Zooming-in on the southeast coast

- Then, after ensuring that the **terrain** object is selected, go to the **Inspector** window, and select the **Raise/Lower Terrain** tool, as indicated in the next figure.

Figure 5-20: Selecting the Raise/Lower Terrain tool

- In the **Scene** view, Press the *SHIFT* key, start to drag and drop your mouse on the blue area and modify the brush size to **36** if necessary (to cover a wider area). As you do so, you will notice chunks of the terrain disappearing, revealing the scene gridlines as described in the next figure. By pressing the *SHIFT* key you can lower the terrain; if you omit to do so, dragging and dropping the mouse will have the opposite effect. So make sure you keep the *SHIFT* key pressed for these actions.

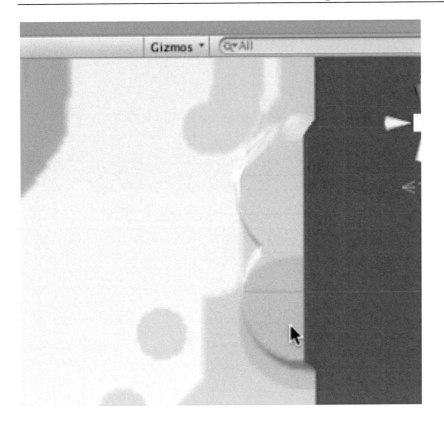

Figure 5-21: Lowering the terrain

- Carry on until you have covered most of the water area around the island.

Once you have completed the entire outline for the island, we can smooth out the edges to make it look a bit neater and polish-up our work.

- After ensuring that the **Terrain** object has been selected, select the **Smooth Height** tool from the **Inspector**, as highlighted on the next figure.

Figure 5-22: Selecting the Smooth Height tool

- Select the second brush from the left-hand side, and set the brush size to **36**. You can also use other settings if you wish to experiment.

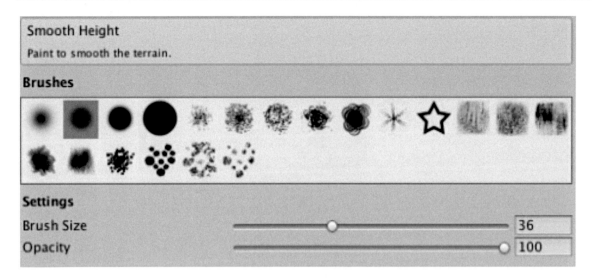

Figure 5-23: Adjusting the properties of the brush

- After adjusting these settings you can apply the brush to the edges created from the previous tool, and you will notice that these are nicely smoothed out.

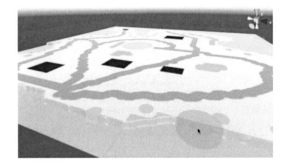

Figure 5-24: The island before the Smooth tool

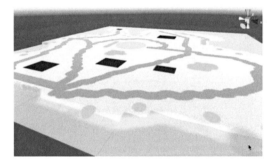

Figure 5-25: The island after the Smooth tool

ADDING WATER

At this stage, the outline has been applied and the boundary between the island and the water is clearly defined. So we can now introduce the water asset. In the next steps, we will successively add the water asset to the scene and adjust it to ensure that the scene is realistic:

- In the **Project** window, go to the folder: **Standard Assets | Environment | Water | Water | Prefabs**.

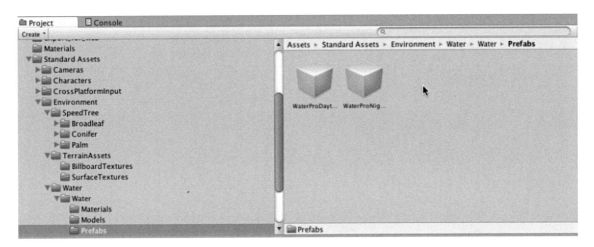

Figure 5-26: Locating the prefab for the water

- Once you have located this folder, you should see two prefabs (blue cubes) within.

- We will be using the prefab labeled **WaterProDaytime**: drag and drop this prefab to the **Scene** view; this will create a new object in the scene (**WaterProDaytime**).

- Using the **Move** tool, move the water object to the center of the map: because in this particular case, we just want to move it along the x- and z-axes, you can either drag these individually or drag and drop the green area defined by these two axes, this will ensure that the object is moved only along the x- and z-axes (i.e., the object will be moved horizontally).

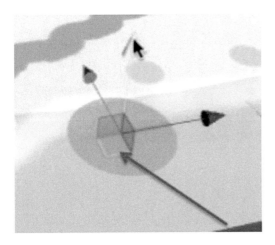

Figure 5-27: Adding water

- Scale-up this object on the **x-** and **z**-axes by **500** (i.e., **x** and **z** scale properties set to **500**)

- Move this object up so that it appears at the boundary that you have just smoothed-out previously (see the boundary highlighted on the next figure): this will take some readjusting and you don't need to have it right the first time. In fact, if some blue color (from the texture of the ground) still appears above the water, we will be able to erase it later on, and replace it by a texture that is similar to the sand instead.

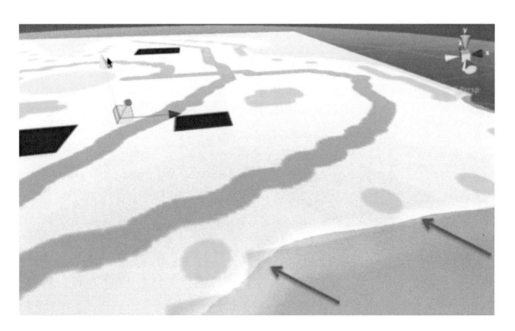

Figure 5-28: Identifying the boundary between the water and the sand

ADDING TREES

Now that the outline has been completed and the water added, it is time to add some more life to the island, including trees and foliage. In the next steps, we will learn how to add trees to the terrain.

- After selecting the **terrain** object in the **Hierarchy** view, select the tool labeled **Place Trees**, as described on the next figure.

Figure 5-29: Selecting the Place Trees tool

- Scroll down within the **Inspector** window.

- In the **Terrain** section, click on the button labeled **Edit Trees**, and then select **Add Tree** from the contextual menu.

Figure 5-30: Editing the trees

- This should open a new window labeled **Add Tree**.

- We need to select the type of tree to be added as there are none selected at present.

- Click on the button to the right of the label **None (Game Object)**, as highlighted on the next figure.

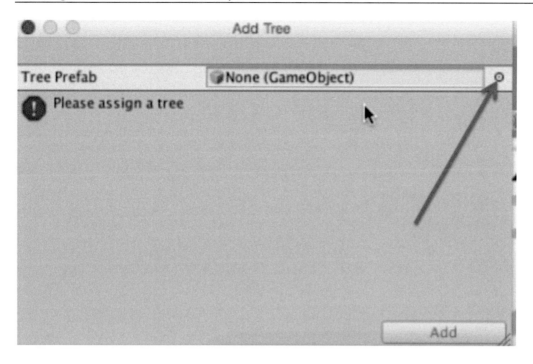

Figure 5-31: Assigning a new tree

- A new window will appear so that you can search for and select a particular type of tree.

- In this new window, type the word **palm** in the search field located at the top of the window; Unity should find a texture called **PalmDesktop**, as illustrated on the next figure.

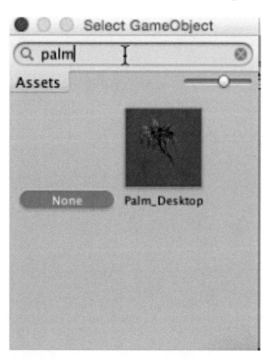

Figure 5-32: Assigning a new tree (continued)

- Click on this texture, this will select the tree and take you back to the previous window.

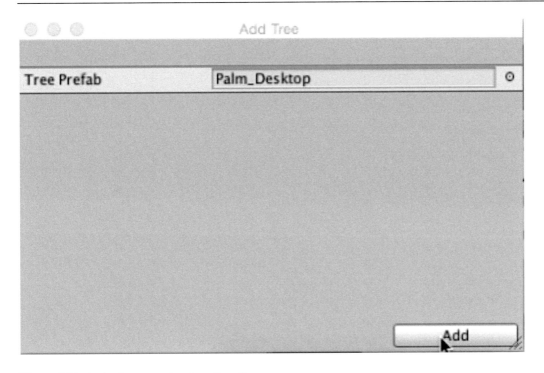

Figure 5-33: Assigning a new tree (continued)

- You should see that **Palm_Desktop** has been selected as the **Tree Prefab**; in other words, we will be able to add trees based on the type or template (or prefab) **Palm_Desktop**.

- We can now click on the button **Add**.

- You should now be able to see that a new type of tree has been added to the **Terrain**.

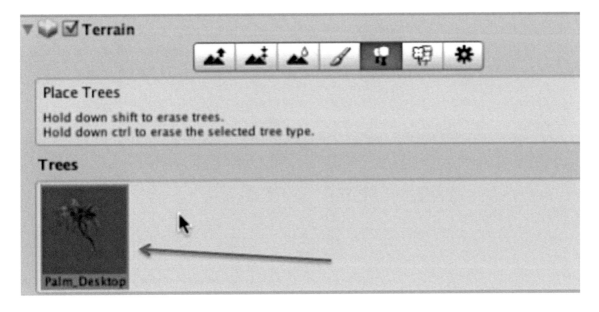

Figure 5-34: Checking available trees to be added to the terrain

At this stage, we are almost ready to add trees to the island. Before you do so, you could modify some of the settings such as **Tree Density** or **Tree Height** (or do so at a later stage).

- In the **Scene** view, locate the green circles that correspond to the location of the trees.

- Click on these (you can also drag the mouse) to add trees.

Figure 5-35: Adding trees to the island

- If you want to add more trees in one go, you can increase the **Trees Density** parameter, and this will speed-up the process.

- If you need to delete trees, just press the *SHIFT* key as you drag the mouse.

- Proceed to the rest of the island and add trees in the areas delimited by green circles or any other location of your choice.

- Try different heights for the trees to see how the settings for the trees affect their appearance.

After adding a few trees, we can now have a look at the scene, and navigate through it. To do so, we just need to add a controller as we have done in the previous chapters:

- In the **Project** view, go to the folder: **Assets|Standard Assets|Characters|FirstPersonCharacter|Prefabs**.

- Locate the prefab labeled **FPSController**.

- Drag and drop this prefab on the scene.

- This will create a new object called **FPSController**.

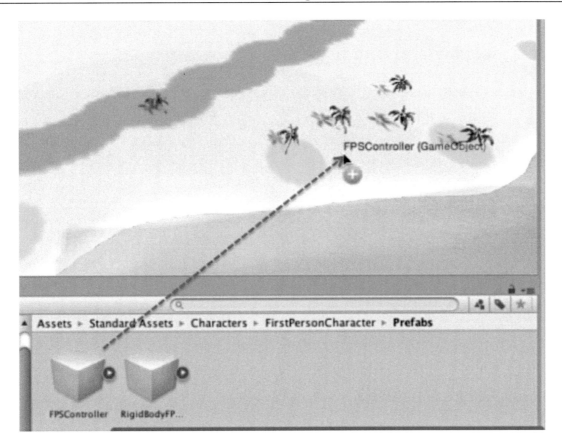

Figure 5-36: Adding a first-person controller

You can then adjust the position of this object so that it is slightly above the ground, and play the scene. The scene should look like the following.

Figure 5-37: Walking around the island

PAINTING THE ISLAND WITH REALISTIC TEXTURES

At this point, the water has been added, along with trees. This being said, while the original design is great, it would be good to be able to paint the terrain using additional textures or even erase some of the green circles or other textures included in the outline. Thankfully, Unity includes a **Paint** tool that makes it possible to literarily paint on the terrain using either built-in textures (e.g., rock, dirt, etc.) or textures that you have already imported. For painting, we dispose of, as for other tools, a wide range of brushes, and we can also adjust its settings (e.g., opacity). So let's jazz-up the look of the island and add some textures to it:

- Select the **Terrain** object in the **Hierarchy** view.

- In the **Inspector** window, select the tool labeled **Paint Texture**, as illustrated on the next figure.

Figure 5-38: Selecting the Paint Texture tool

Again, we will need to add a particular texture to this paint brush; as a result, we will click on the button labeled **Edit Texture**, and then on the option **Add Texture** from the contextual menu.

- As for previously, click on the button labeled **Edit Texture**, and select **Add Texture** from the contextual menu: this will make it possible to edit the texture to be applied on the terrain.

- A new window called **Add Terrain Texture** will appear.

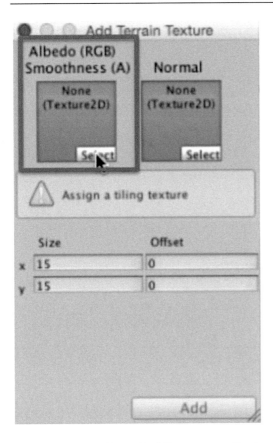

Figure 5-39: Selecting and adding a texture for the terrain

- Click on the **Select** button for the **Albedo (RGB)**.

- A new window will appear in which you can search for and select the texture **GrassRockyAlbedo** (click once on the texture).

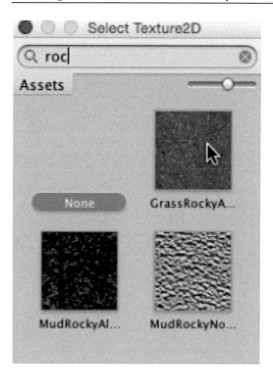

Figure 5-40: Selecting and adding a texture for the terrain

- Once this is done, you will be back to the previous window; it will show that the texture has been selected.

- You can keep the default values for the size of the texture (i.e., **15 by 15**).

- Click on the button **Add**.

- In the **Inspector** window, you should now see that the texture has been added to the available textures for the terrain.

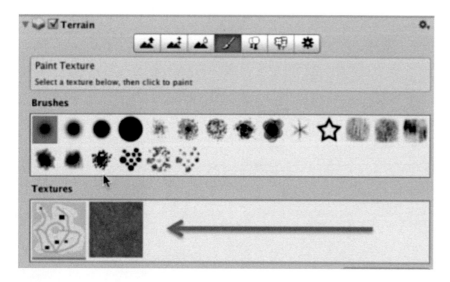

Figure 5-41: Selecting the new texture to paint

- As for previously, we can adjust the **Brush Size** and **Opacity**. I have set my settings to **17** and **100** respectively, but I invite you to experiment and see what works best for you.

- Finally, select (i.e., click on) the texture of your choice in the **Inspector** window, in the section **Textures**, so that the texture is applied to the brush.

- Drag the mouse (i.e., left-click and move) around the area where you want to apply this texture in the **Scene** view.

Figure 5-42: Applying a texture to the terrain

At this stage, you can start painting other areas on the island; we could also, for example, erase parts of the island, that we would like to amend. You can of course use *CTRL+Z* to undo any of your previous actions; however, if you would like to remove an image or an item that is part of the outline map, you can proceed differently by erasing or painting over it using the color of the sand. This can be done easily as follows:

- Locate the file **sandy_color.jpg** in your file system (i.e., where you imported the necessary assets for this chapter).

- Import the file **sandy_color.jpg** into your project by dragging and dropping this file from your file system (e.g., explorer or Finder) to the **Assets** window in Unity.

- Once this is done, select the **Terrain** object in the **Hierarchy** view.

- Repeat the steps performed in the previous section to add this texture to the list of available textures for the **Paint Texture** tool.

- Once this is done, select the sand texture to paint, as illustrated on the next figure.

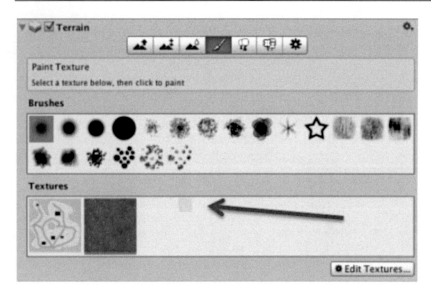

Figure 5-43: Selecting the sandy texture to erase parts of the island

- Start to paint over the **Terrain**, for example on the path, and you should notice that it disappears progressively, as illustrated on the next figure.

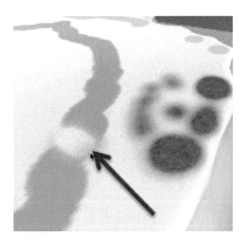

Figure 5-44: Applying the sandy texture

- Using this method, you can delete any of the textures introduced by the map overlay.

Figure 5-45: Before erasing

Figure 5-46: After erasing

After deleting some of the original path, you can then apply, instead, textures that you have already defined in Unity.

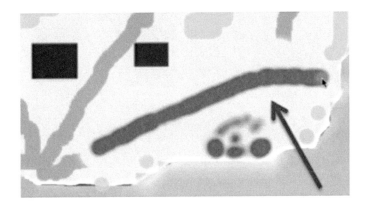

Figure 5-47: Applying a new texture to the path

Adding Foliage

In addition to creating trees, Unity also makes it possible to add foliage (e.g., plants), that increase the realism of your scene. They can be, as for the trees, included using a corresponding tool. Let's add some foliage to the scene:

- Select the **Terrain** object in the **Hierarchy** view.

- In the **Inspector**, in the **Terrain** section, select the **Paint Details** tool as illustrated on the next figure.

Figure 5-48: Selecting the Paint Details tool

In the section called **Details**, click on the button labeled **Edit Details**, and then select the option **Add Grass Texture** from the contextual menu.

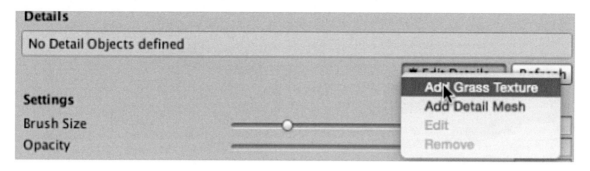

Figure 5-49: Adding the texture for the grass

- A new window labeled **Add Grass Texture** will appear; as you will see, no texture has been selected yet, so we will look for and select a texture for our foliage.

- Click on the button to the right of the label **None(Texture2D)** as described on the next figure.

- This should display a search window: enter the text **grass** in the search field and then select the texture labeled **GrassFrond02** from the results.

- Once this is done, a new window will appear, this time with the texture that you have selected.

- Press **Add** to add this texture.

- The full process is summarized on the next figure.

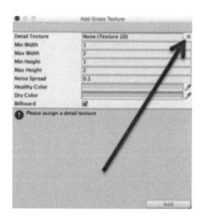

Figure 5-50: Adding a texture for the grass (step 1)

Figure 5-51: Adding a texture for the grass (step 2)

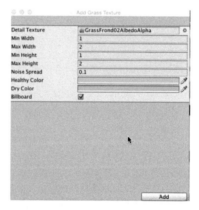

Figure 5-52: Adding a texture for the grass (step 3)

- At this stage, the next texture should appear in the section labeled **Details.**

- You can now add foliage to the island. I have used the following settings (but feel free to experiment with different values): **Brush size = 20, Opacity = 1, Target Strength = 0.8**

Figure 5-53: A portion of the island with foliage from the scene view

Once you have completed your modifications on parts of the island, play the scene and observe the foliage.

Figure 5-54: A portion of the island with foliage from the game view

ADDING A LAKE AND A MOUNTAIN

In terms of realism, we have managed to add some pretty interesting features, including trees, foliage, water, and textures. One of the last elements that we need to add is the lake that is located in the middle of the map as well as a mountain. For both elements, we will need to either carve into the terrain (to lower the terrain) or raise the terrain, and we will be using the tool **Raise/Lower Terrain** for this purpose.

- Select the **Terrain** object in the **Hierarchy** view.

- Pan the view *(CTRL + Q)* so that the lake appears in the middle of the view.

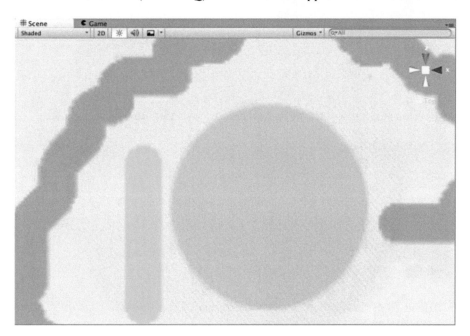

Figure 5-55: Locating the lake

- In the **Inspector** window, select the **Raise/Lower Terrain** tool (first icon from the left).

If you are not sure about the name of the icons located in the toolbar for the terrain, you can move the mouse over any of these icons, and a tooltip (i.e., contextual label) will display the name of the corresponding tool.

- Select the third brush from the left. This size should be appropriate to carve the lake, but feel free to use other brushes if they work better for you.

- Select a brush size of **51** and set the opacity to **84**.

- Press the *SHIFT* key, left-click (i.e., press the mouse's left button), and then drag your mouse (i.e., move) on top of the blue area that defines the lake.

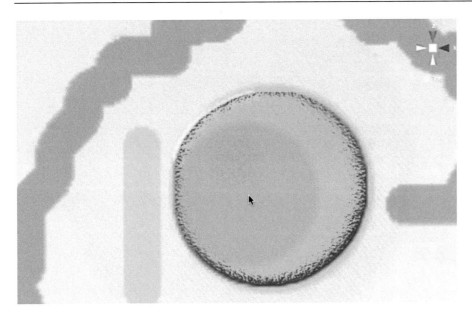

Figure 5-56: Defining the lake

- Using the **Smooth Height** tool, smooth out the boundary of the lake.

- So that we can observe this area with the **First-Person Controller**, move the **First-Person Controller** close to the boundary of the lake and play the scene.

Figure 5-57: Looking at the lake

- Once this is done, we will now create a simple hill using the same tool; we will be creating a hill close to the lake in the area highlighted on the next figure.

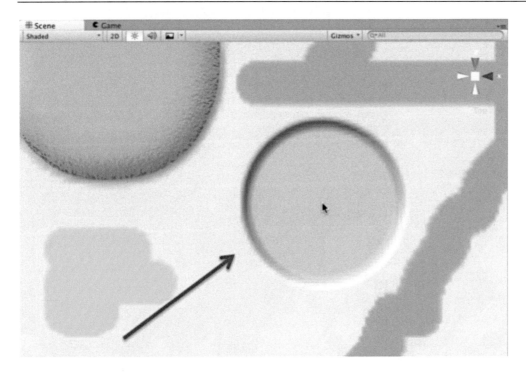

Figure 5-58: Locating the position of the hill

- You can stop to play the scene.

- In the **Inspector** window, select the **Raise/Lower Terrain** tool (first icon from the left).

- Select the third brush from the left. This size should be most appropriate to carve the lake but feel free to use other brushes if it works better for you.

- Select a brush size of **51** and set the opacity to **84**.

- Click the *Left Mouse Button*, and then drag and drop the mouse on top of the blue area that we identified earlier, as per the next figure.

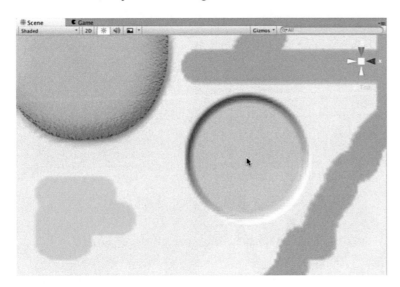

Figure 5-59: Creating a hill (part1)

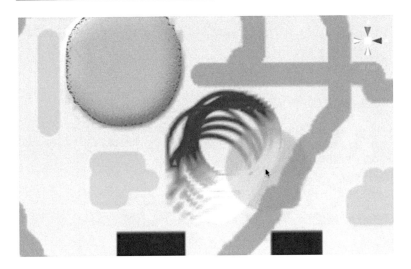

Figure 5-60: Creating a hill (part 2)

After these modifications, you can pan your view to check that you have managed to raise the ground properly, and it should look as follows (although this could take many iterations, so it's perfectly ok if it does not look exactly like the next image). Also, remember that you can undo your actions using *CTRL + Z,* if need be.

Figure 5-61: Viewing the hill from above

At this stage, we just need to apply a texture to the mountain to make it look more realistic. As for the ground, we will be using the paint tool after selecting an appropriate texture:

- Select the object labeled **Terrain** in the **Hierarchy** view, and use the following settings: **brush size= 51, Opacity = 84, Target Strength = 1.**

- Select the fourth brush from the left.

- Select the tool **Paint Texture** as well as the second texture in the list (i.e., **GrassFrond02**), as described on the next figure.

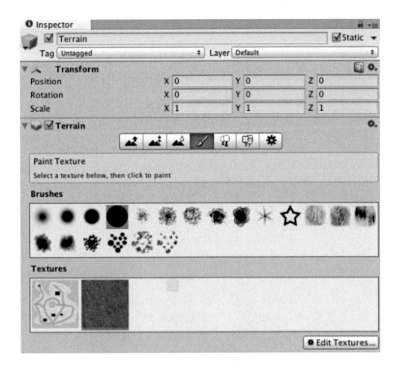

Figure 5-62: Selecting and using the Paint Texture tool

- You can now paint the hill; you can either keep the default view in the **Scene** view or switch to a top-down view by clicking on the **y-axis** of the **gizmo**.

- To paint the border of the mountain, you can use different settings for the brush (e.g., **Opacity=64**).

- Once you have finished painting the hill, it should look like the one illustrated on the next figure.

Figure 5-63: The hill viewed from above

- Play your scene to see how the hill looks like in the **Game** window.

Figure 5-64: The hill viewed in the game view

Of course, the hill that you have created may look slightly different, and that is perfectly ok.

Note that you can always undo any of your design using *CTRL + Z* or by lowering the areas that you have previously raised (by pressing the *SHIFT* key when using the **Raise/Lower Terrain** tool).

ADDING A CAR TO THE 3D ENVIRONMENT

So at this stage, we have a great environment with trees, foliage, water, and hills. However, due to the size of the island, it may be more convenient for the player to navigate using a car rather than walking. Luckily, Unity includes a set of built-in vehicles that are ready to be used without too much tweaking, except from the addition of a camera. In this section, we will discover how we can import and include these assets into our scene. First, let's import the **Vehicles** package:

- In Unity, select: **Assets | Import Package | Vehicles.**

- A new window labeled **Import Package** will appear.

- Click on **Import** to import all the assets within.

Once the process is complete, we can check that these have been imported properly by going to the folder **Assets | Standard Assets | Vehicles,** and checking that it includes both the folders **Aircraft** and **Car,** as described on the next figure.

Figure 5-65: Folders created for the vehicles

- Go to the folder **Assets | Standard Assets | Vehicles | Car | Prefabs** and drag and drop the asset labeled **Car** from its folder onto the **Scene** view, near the **First-Person Controller.**

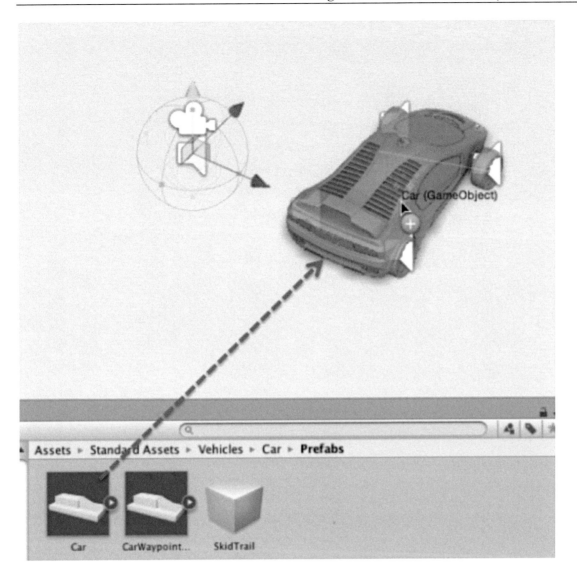

Figure 5-66: Adding the car to the environment

Because we have two controllers in the scene, we will temporarily deactivate the **First-Person Controller** so that using the arrow keys on the keyboard only moves the car, and we will also ensure that the car is now the target of (or is followed by) the main camera.

First let's include a new camera that follows the car:

- Go to the folder **Assets | Standard Assets | Cameras | Prefabs**.

- Select the prefab **FreeLookCameraRig** and drag and drop it to the **Scene** (or the **Hierarchy**) view.

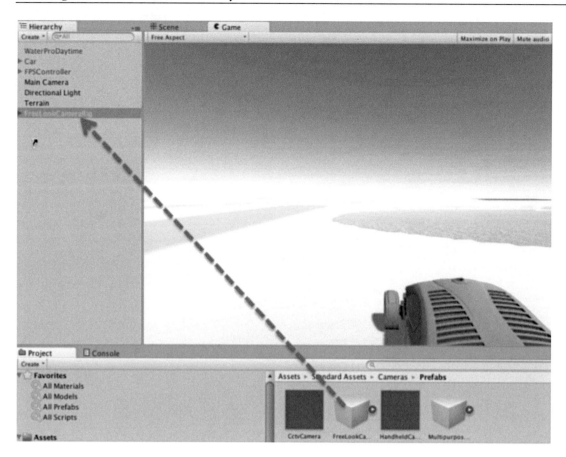

Figure 5-67: Adding a camera to the scene

- Then set the car as the target for this camera by dragging and dropping the object labeled **Car** to the **Target** attribute of the camera, as described on the next figure.

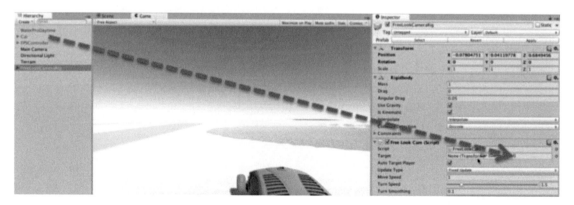

Figure 5-68: Setting the target for the moving camera

- Then, we will deactivate the **First-Person Controller** since it will not be used for navigation. To do so, select the **First-Person Controller** in the scene and, using the **Inspector** window, deactivate this object (uncheck the box as illustrated on the next figure).

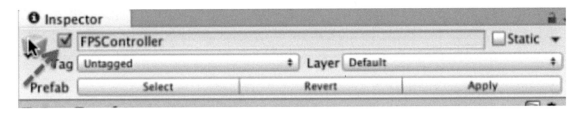

Figure 5-69: Deactivating the FPS Controller

- And last, we will also deactivate the main camera, using the same technique; using the **Inspector** window, deactivate this object (i.e., uncheck the box as illustrated on the next figure).

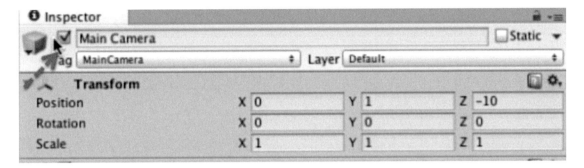

Figure 5-70: Deactivating the main camera

Once this is done, you should be able to play the scene, and see the car moving as you press the arrow keys (i.e., up, down, left and right to respectively, accelerate, decelerate, turn left or turn right).

Figure 5-71: Driving the car

ADDING AN AIRCRAFT TO THE ENVIRONMENT

As mentioned earlier, Unity offers several types of vehicles, including a car and an aircraft. In this section, we will focus on adding and piloting an aircraft to fly over the island and see it from the sky.

First let's add the aircraft:

- In Unity, go to the folder **Assets | Standard Assets | Vehicles | AirCraft | Prefabs** and drag and drop the asset labeled **AircraftJet** from its folder onto the **Scene** view, near the **First-Person Controller**.

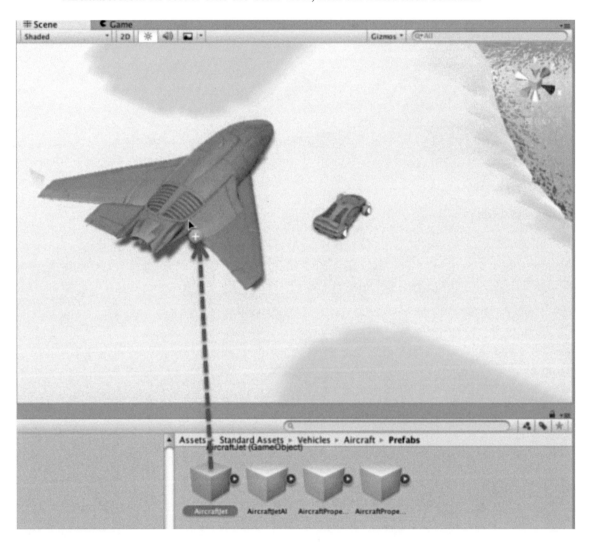

Figure 5-72: Adding the aircraft to the scene

- Then, we will deactivate the object labeled **Car** since we will not be using it for navigation. To do so, select the **Car** in the **Scene** view and, using the **Inspector**, deactivate this object (uncheck the box as illustrated on the next figure).

Figure 5-73: Deactivating the car

- Finally, we will set the aircraft as the target for the active camera by dragging and dropping the object labeled **AircraftJet** to the **Target** attribute of the active camera (i.e., **FreelookCameraRig**), as described on the next figure.

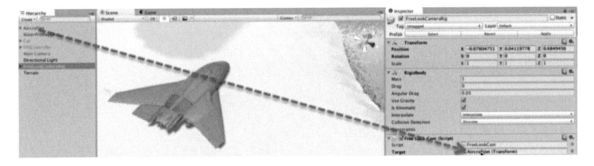

Figure 5-74: Setting the aircraft as the target of the camera

Once this is done, you should be able to play the scene, and pilot the aircraft by pressing the arrow keys on your keyboard (down arrow to go up).

Figure 5-75: Piloting the aircraft

ADDING ONBOARD CAMERAS TO THE AIRCRAFT

In the previous section, while we have managed to add and pilot the aircraft, the camera may sometimes not be fast enough to follow the aircraft; also, it would be great to see the virtual world from within the cockpit or as if you were looking down. To achieve this, we will successively add two cameras: one that is in the cockpit and that looks forward, and another camera that looks down and that reveals a view of the island from the sky.

Let's add the first camera:

- Create a new camera: select **GameObject|Camera** from the top menu.

- This will create a new object labeled **Camera** in the **Hierarchy** view.

- Drag and drop this camera atop the object **AircraftJet** object. This way, the camera is now a child of the plane. In other words, any transformation applied to the plane will be applied to the camera; so as the plane will be moving, so will the (embedded) camera.

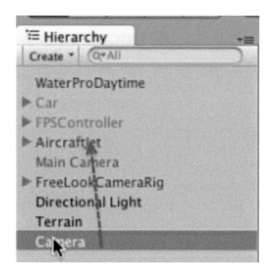
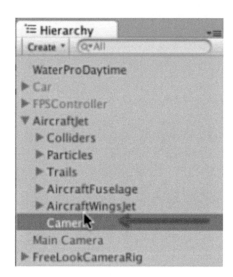

Figure 5-76: Setting the camera as a child of the aircraft

Figure 5-77: The camera listed as a child of the aircraft

- You can then rename this camera, for example, **from_plane**

When this is done, we need to change the position of the camera so that it is located at the front of the plane, inside the cockpit.

> The position of any child object is usually provided in relation to its parent. For example, if the parent is at the position (4, 5, 6) and the child's position is (1,0,0), it means that the child is at the position (1,0,0) in relation to the parent. In other word, its relative position is (1,0,0) but its absolute position (in the game environment) is **(4, 5, 6) + (1, 0, 0)** which is **(5,5,6)**.

With this in mind, we can change the position of the camera to **(0,1.5,7.0)** as illustrated in the next figure.

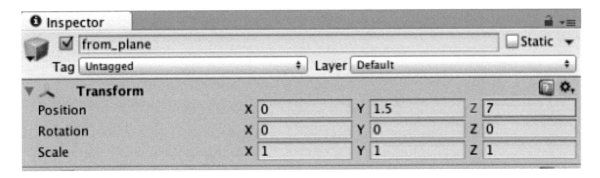

Figure 5-78: Positioning the camera within the aircraft

To ensure that the camera is positioned properly, we can check the view from this camera in the bottom-right corner of the **Scene** view.

Figure 5-79: Checking the position of the camera

Before we can play the scene, we will need to deactivate the camera that we have used so far (**FreeLookCameraRig**) using the **Inspector** window.

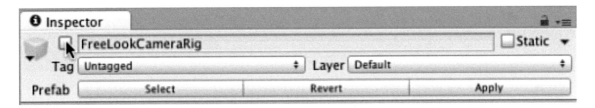

Figure 5-80: Deactivating the current camera

As we play the scene and take off from the island, we can see the view from the cockpit as described in the next figure.

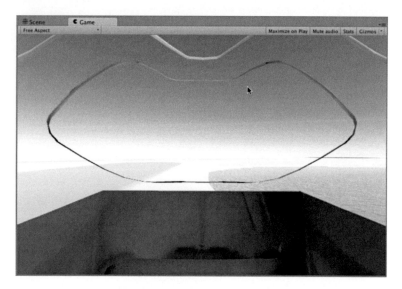

Figure 5-81: The view from the cockpit

The last change we need to apply now is the addition of a camera that looks down from the airplane; for this purpose, we can use the same principle as previously, by creating a new camera; the only difference is that we will display the image captured by this camera atop the current view (i.e., similar to an additional screen in the cockpit).

Let's add the second camera:

- Create a new camera: Select **GameObject|Camera** from the top menu.

- This will create a new object labeled **Camera** in the **Hierarchy** view.

- Drag and drop this camera atop the object **AircraftJet**.

- Rename this camera **looking_down**.

- Select this object (i.e., **looking_down**).

- In the **Inspector** window, locate the **Transform** section: change the **position** of this object to **(0, 0, 0)** and the **rotation** to **(90, 0, 0)**: this rotates the camera around the **x-axis** about 90 degrees so that it is oriented downwards.

- In the **Inspector** window, locate the **Camera** component for this object. In the subsection labeled **ViewPort Rect**, change the settings to **W=3 and H=3**. Keep the x and y settings to (0,0).

- In the **Depth** subsection, enter the value **2**.

The **ViewPort Rect** describes where the image captured by the camera should be displayed. This image is displayed in a rectangle defined by its position (x, y) and size (width and height). The width and height are representing a percentage of the screen (e.g., 1 for 100%). The x and y coordinates define the bottom-left corner of the rectangle, with (0,0) being the bottom left corner of the **Scene** view. All cameras also have a depth, and the camera with the higher depth is displayed on top of cameras with lower depths. In this example, because other cameras have a depth of **0** by default, the image captured by this camera will be displayed on top of the images captured by the other cameras, and can therefore be seen as part of the interface.

As you play the scene and take off from the island, you should see the shadow of the aircraft on the water, captured by the second camera, displayed in the bottom-left corner of the view, as illustrated on the next figure.

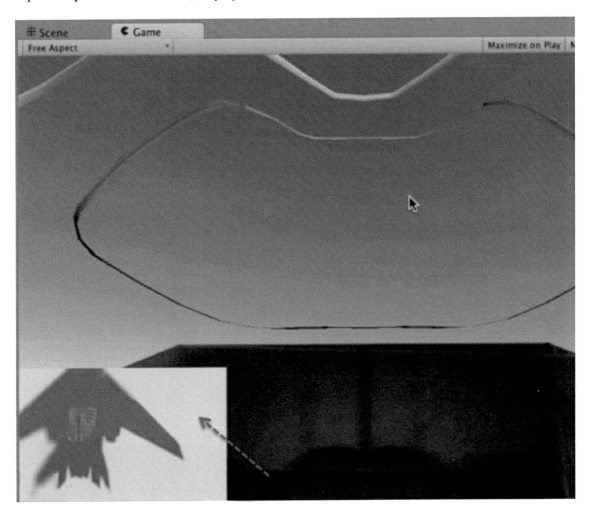

Figure 5-82: View from the second embedded camera

Note that to have the time to see the ground from the second camera (i.e., embedded camera looking downwards), we could create other islands by duplicating the **Terrain** several times, and moving the duplicates along the **z-axis**, as illustrated on the next picture.

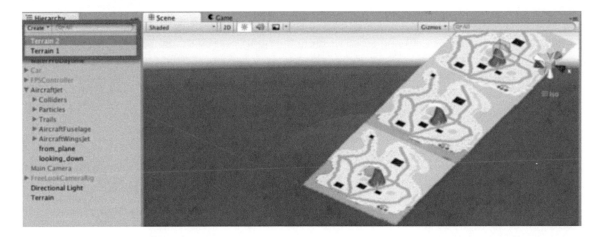

Figure 5-83: Duplicating the island

As you play the scene, you will have more time to see the islands from the camera labeled **looking_down**.

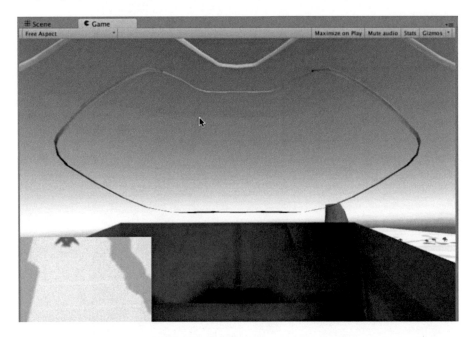

Figure 5-84: Seeing the islands from the cockpit

ADDING BUILDINGS TO THE ISLAND

We have, at this stage, added all the necessary elements to our island, based on our outline, except from the buildings. These can be created very easily using the same techniques covered in the previous chapters, as you will need to:

- Create new boxes.

- Place and resize these boxes so that they cover the black areas on the outline.

- Scale these boxes on the **y-axis**, using a height of your choice (for example **40**).

Finally, we can add a texture to the buildings. As for previously, you can import a texture, from the resources previously downloaded, called **buildings.jpg**, and then drag and drop it on one of the buildings. You can then modify the tiling for this texture to **(1, 5)** by accessing its corresponding material. This being said, you can use any texture of your choice, including the texture that you have already applied to the tiles for the indoor environment.

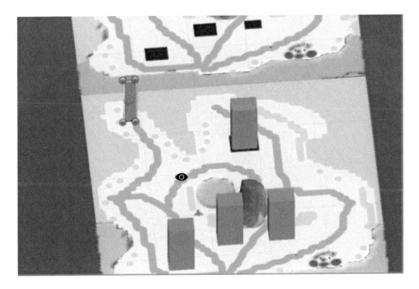

Figure 5-85: Adding buildings to the first island

While we have only created the buildings for the first island, you can easily duplicate them twice and position the duplicates on the two additional islands. After adding the buildings, you can play the scene and check how each of them looks like by either:

- Walking around the island after deactivating all character and vehicle controllers (except for the **First-Person Controller**) as well as the camera **FreeLookCameraRig** that follows these controllers.

- Driving around the island by deactivating all controllers (except for the **Car**), and activating the **FreeLookCameraRig** camera and setting its target accordingly.

- Flying around the island by deactivating all controllers (except for the **AircraftJet**).

Figure 5-86: The island with a building

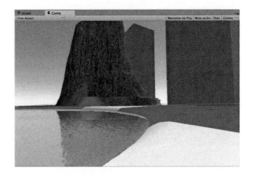

Figure 5-87: Walking around the island

LEVEL ROUNDUP

Summary

In this chapter, we have become more comfortable with the creation of indoor and outdoor environments and we learned how to use Unity's built-in assets to create an impressive environment. We delved into the different tools available in Unity to create, transform and texture basic shapes. Well, from finding your way around Unity to creating a realistic island, you can see that you have already made some considerable progress since the start of the book. You have managed to combine your skills, yet with no programming knowledge, to create a truly realistic and interactive environment.

Quiz

It is now time to test your knowledge. Please answer the following questions (e.g., Yes or No). The answers are available on the companion website (http://www.learntocreategames.com/learn-unity-ebook).

1. A viewport is a circular area that defines where the content captured by a camera will be displayed onscreen.

2. The position of a child object is always determined based on the position of the parent.

3. Once a terrain has been created it can't be modified.

4. It is possible to create a mountain (hill) with Unity.

5. It is necessary to flatten a terrain before raising or lowering any area within.

6. The package called **Environment** includes all necessary assets to create water and trees.

7. Once trees have been created they can't be removed.

8. It is possible to create a terrain with hills and valleys from a simple box object.

9. The content of only one camera can be displayed onscreen.

10. The content of a camera always fills-up the entire screen.

Checklist

If you can do the following, then you are ready to go to the next chapter:

*   Create a terrain.

*   Raise and lower parts of the terrain.

*   Add foliage, trees and water to the terrain.

*   Add (and track) a car or an airplane that includes an embedded camera.

*   Combine the output of several cameras onscreen.

Challenge 1

For this challenge, you will need to create a new outdoor environment, based on a new template as follows:

*   Import the texture **gameOutline2.png** from the folders that you have downloaded from the companion site.

*   Create a new scene.

*   Apply the same techniques as before to recreate the island.

*   Add vehicles of your choice.

Challenge 2

For this challenge, you will need to create your own outline, using the image manipulation tool of your choice, and then apply it to create a new island of your own design!

You could proceed as follows:

- Create a new image with a size of 500 pixels by 500 pixels.

- Set the background to white.

- Create the outline of the island using a brush of size 1.

- Add green, blue, or brown areas to identify the position of trees, water, or paths.

- Save your image in the **jpg** or **png** format.

- Import this image into Unity.

- Create a new scene.

- Use this new template to create you new outdoor scene.

6
FREQUENTLY ASKED QUESTIONS

This chapter provides answers to the most frequently asked questions about the features that we have covered in this book.

NAVIGATION

How do I navigate through my scene?

Import the **Characters** assets and add one of the built-in controllers to the scene.

After importing my FPSController and adding it to the scene, it looks like it is falling as I play the scene.

Make sure that the **FPSController** is above the ground when added to the scene.

After importing my FPSController I walk around the Island but I only see the scene from a static camera.

Make sure that the main camera is deactivated.

After creating my maze, I can still see around my character although no lights are active in the scene?

Make sure that you have set the ambient light for the scene to an intensity of 0 (**Window|Lighting**).

TRANSFORMATIONS AND ASSETS

How do I import assets in my scene?

Import the asset (e.g., texture, image or sound) by selecting **Assets > Import Assets**. For textures, you then just need to drag-and-drop the texture on your object. You can also drag and drop the assets from your file system (e.g., explorer or Finder) into Unity.

Where are my assets stored in my project?

Usually, assets are saved or imported in the active folder. So if the active folder (the one selected in the **Project** window) is **Assets**, then the assets will be imported in this folder (excepts for most of Unity's built-in assets that will be, by default, imported in the folder **Standard Assets**).

How can I transform objects?

You can select the object and then either use the key shortcuts (i.e., W, E, R, and T) or modify the object's transform properties in the **Inspector** window.

What is the difference between the Rect tool and the Scale tool?

The **Rect** tool was introduced in Unity 5. But before then, if you scaled an object, let's say a cube, its position would be changed as well. So, for example when you were designing a maze with boxes, you would constantly need to scale the boxes, and then move the box to compensate for the scale transformation. With the **Rect** tool, all is all taken care of, so as you resize the object with the **Rect** tool, at least two of its corners will remain at the same position.

CREATING, ORGANISING AND SEARCHING FOR OBJECTS AND ASSETS

How do I create an object?

Select: **GameObject|Add**.

How do I add a texture?

Import the texture (**Assets|Import Assets**) and drag-and-drop it to your object.

How do I group objects?

Create an empty object (parent) and drag-and-drop the objects to be grouped on the parent.

How do I look for objects in my project?

Use the project search window and search by name or type (e.g., **t:scene**)

If I import an asset in my project, can I access it from any scene within this project?

Yes, and that's a very interesting feature that will save some space on your hard drive.

7
THANK YOU

I would like to thank you for completing this book; I trust that you are now confortable with Unity and that you can create interactive 3D game environments. This book is the first in a series of four books on Unity 5, so it may be time to move on to the next book for the beginner level where you will learn more about scripting. You can find a description of this book on the official page http://www.learntocreategames.com/learn-unity-ebook.

So that the book can be constantly improved, I would really appreciate your feedback and hear what you have to say. So, please leave me a helpful review on Amazon letting me know what you thought of the book and also send me an email (learntocreategames@gmail.com) with any suggestion you may have. I read and reply to every email.

Thanks so much!!

Made in the USA
San Bernardino, CA
10 January 2017